THE

Ancient

PATH

SECOND EDITION

Also *by* Norman Willis

THE *Ancient* PATH*II*

Norman Willis

A Return *to the* Kingdom Mandate
of Generational Transfer

Christ Church Publishing®

Unless otherwise noted, all scripture references are taken from The Holy Bible, The New International Version, Copyright © 1978 by New York International Bible Society Publishers. Used by permission.

Second Printing 1999
Third Printing   2006

Christ Church Publishing.
11725 NE 118th St, Kirkland, WA 98034
www.cckirkland.org

Summary: The Ancient Path is a passionate cry to both generations that enables us to see the biblical mandate of generational transfer and then practically describes how that transfer is to occur.

ISBN #0–96424–877–8

Design Team: by Paul Graves, with Michael Bailey, Roseanne Hallstrom and Christine Heric

CONTENTS

PART *I*

PART *II*

THE

Ancient

PATH[II]

PART *1*

To me generational transfer is when a person who could be a mentor, hero, or teacher, puts a desire into another person to follow and act in his footsteps.

Generational transfer is happening this very day. For example, my father has put a desire into me to take the baton when he retires. He has put into me a will with a destiny to carry Christ Church Kirkland when I grow up. God is enabling me to see the vision and share this passion with my father.

Generational transfer is something I am glad God made so I can feel the things my father does. Psalm 22:30 says, "Posterity will serve him and future generations will be told about the Lord." To me that means, I will know and respect who my father is in the Lord. My father and God are giving me the vision to see, with spiritual eyes, who I am in the Lord. Generational transfer is transforming my life in ways that people in other generations did not receive. Ephesians 3:5 says, it "was not made known to men in other generations..." I am blessed that my father has inspired me and blessed me with Jesus. With generational transfer, we can have dominion over worldly and corrupt generations. Psalm 145:13 says, "Your Kingdom is an everlasting Kingdom and Your dominion endures throughout all generations." I know God wants the generations of His people to impart generational transfer to their children.

BY KYLE WILLIS, *October 1998*

It is a true blessing and honor to compose an endorsement for such a man of God like Pastor Norm Willis.

This book is what God has been speaking in my spirit transiently, and God has used Pastor Willis to bring confirmation in my life.

The Ancient Path is the book every God fearing man and woman should not only read, but practice. The concepts of this book are very perceptible in their teaching in what we need to return to transferring the Spirit of God to the next four generations.

Men and women who are truly hearing the voice of God are not only concerned about this present generation but also the generation to come. This book echoes the voice of God in such an intense manner that you can not help but see the Kingdom of God being manifested through generational transfer.

Pastor Willis, thank you for having Kingdom insight and a sensitive ear to hear the call for us to take responsibility for the next generation. Those of us who have sincere love for our children do not want to see the next generation start from ground zero. Therefore, we need this book in our library to help us become men and women who transfer every godly aspect of our lives to the next generation.

We need to make sure that there is a spiritual transfer left in our children, so that there will be godly leaders in our churches, community, and government. If we fail to take the principles in this book and activate them in our lives, we will have failed the mandate of God. If we fail to use these principles, we will fail to leave this country with godly successors for positions of authority. Therefore, I encourage all men and women of God to get this book and deposit into future leaders of this great country.

Thank you again,

Bishop Eddie L. Long, D.D., D.H.L
Senior Pastor, New Birth Missionary Baptist Church

INTRODUCTION

THE LIEUTENANT GOVERNOR OF THE STATE OF WASHINGTON had
invited me to sit in his chair of civil authority. There I sat with utter amaze-
ment at what I had just witnessed. I had been asked to attend and open that
day's session of the Senate in prayer. As it was every morning, opening
prayer was scheduled to begin promptly at nine o'clock. As I waited for
9:00 to appear on my watch, the Lieutenant Governor leaned over to me
and said, "Don't worry if there are no senators here when you pray.
Though the session officially opens at nine each morning, roll call isn't
until nine-thirty, so that's when they plan to arrive." It was exactly as he had
said. From nine o'clock until nine-nineteen, there were only one or two senators present. At 9:19AM it looked as if floodgates had been opened. By
exactly 9:20AM all the senators had arrived!

After the opening prayer, the Lieutenant Governor invited me to sit in his
chair of authority and observe the session. It was from that chair of civil
authority that I came to the startling conclusion, "There is no government
in government." As I sat observing this ship we call state, I discovered no
one is at the helm. No one is steering the ship.

As the session continued, various senators would take the floor to describe
various aspects of their bill's agenda. As they did, I observed no one was
paying attention. Their fellow senators were busy with their own concerns;
the Lieutenant Governor was leaning over talking to me. At one point
someone had to come and pull on the coat tail of the Lieutenant Governor
to get his attention, so he could answer the senator who had the floor.

CONFIRMING THE VISION

It was there in that chair of civil authority that my vision for the coming generations was confirmed. With no authority at the helm to lead, leadership is an open door of opportunity. Where there is a void of leadership and authority, someone will in fact seize the opportunity to exert their power. And those who seize the power will lead. Those who lead will propagate their agenda, either for good or for evil.

The questions facing any position of leadership:
> By whose authority do you lead?
> By whose authority do you function?
> By whose authority do you validate your expectations?

"Be fruitful and increase in number; fill the earth and subdue it. Rule over the fish of the sea and the birds of the air and over every living creature that moves on the ground." (Genesis 1:28)

A vision for generational transfer is rooted in the issue of authority and commission. In the void of leadership, who is better to fill the vacuum than those who have been duly authorized and commissioned by Almighty God to rule over every living creature that moves on the ground?

"The earth is the Lord's and the fullness thereof." (Psalm 24:1). It is to His sons and daughters that God delegates the positions of leadership in every jurisdictional sphere of life. Because He is sovereign, He reserves the right to delegate these positions for His own. He will insure that those in positions of authority will not only rule *for* Him, but even more importantly, will rule *like* Him.

A VISION FOR GENERATIONAL TRANSFER

A vision for generational transfer begins in the heart of God. Carrying a heart for the generations to come is not a present day fad that was thought up for Himself. God has always had a heart for the generations. Generational transfer is the very means by which He determined His purposes to be extended throughout time.

"He decreed statutes for Jacob and established the law in Israel, which He commanded our forefathers to teach their children, so the next generation would know them, even the children yet to be born, and they in turn would tell their children." (Psalm 78:5-6)

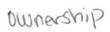

This command to the fathers of Israel covered a span of four generations:
> "Forefathers"   Generation One
> "Their children"   Generation Two
> "Children yet to be born" Generation Three
> "Their children"   Generation Four

In the light of generational transfer, Christianity is always one generation from extinction. If every forefather abdicated his responsibility to transfer, Christianity would cease to be. Obviously God has not permitted that. He will assure that the forefathers continue the generational line.

Simply stated, generational transfer is a vision that sees the way God has ordained for truth and life to be imparted to the coming generations. It is a vision that embraces a responsibility to impart to the generations to come, the life and deposit of Christ given to us.

PURPOSE DEFINED

The purpose of this book is to look strategically into the future and define what is needed. The need, simply defined, yet profound, is the raising of a generation that will not only receive the baton from the fathers who have gone before, but also be stewards of that investment with a vision for the generations that will come after. More specifically, its purpose is to prepare the Joshuas who will receive the mantle of leadership from the Moses' who are now in charge. This book is simply a preceding word that frames for us the need for generational transfer and then defines a clear-cut strategy, particularly in Part II of this book, as to how that transfer is to take place. *"Moses my servant is dead. Now then, you. . ." (Joshua 1:2)* Joshua Chapter One is the account of the generational transfer between Moses and Joshua. It is both God's preceding word of intent and His governmental word of commission. Through intent and commission, God answers two absolutely critical issues facing the generations to come:

> What direction are they to take?
> By whose authority will they function?

The first deals with discernment. The second deals with government.

A Return to the Ancient Path

Once the purpose is defined, one must determine the direction. How is it to be accomplished? The Word of God is our only standard for faith and conduct. Jeremiah provides a clear starting place for us.

"This is what the Lord says: 'Stand at the crossroads and look; ask for the ancient paths, ask where the good way is, and walk in it, and you will find rest for your souls.'" (Jeremiah 6:16)

The church has been living *modern* and now it is time to train *old*. It is time to stand at the crossroads and ask for the ancient path. Those on the ancient path will find the Ancient of Days. It is God who will place in us the heart of a father or the heart of a mother and show us the way of generational transfer.

"...This is my covenant with you: You will be the father of many nations. No longer will you be called Abram; your name will be Abraham, for I have made you a father of many nations. I will make you very fruitful; I will make nations of you, and kings will come from you. I will establish my covenant as an everlasting covenant between me and you and your descendants after you for the generations to come, to be your God and the God of your descendants after you." (Genesis 17:4-7)

This book is a call to responsibility. It is a trumpet call of return, calling us back to the ancient paths of godly desire. It is a call for fathers and mothers to see the way of conquest...the way of generational transfer.

The Spirit of Elijah

The longer I am involved in the process of generational transfer the more I am convinced it is an issue of the heart. If the fathers are unwilling to give their hearts or the sons unwilling to receive the heart given, the fruit of generational transfer will never be produced. *"And he will go on before the Lord, in the spirit and power of Elijah, to turn the hearts of the fathers to their children and the disobedient to the wisdom of the righteous, to make ready a people prepared for the Lord." (Luke 1:17)*

It was the angel of the Lord that said John the Baptist would go before the Lord in the spirit of Elijah. What does it mean to go on before the Lord in the spirit of Elijah? Why the spirit of Elijah? Why not the Spirit of Moses? Moses was perhaps the greatest leader history had ever seen. Why not come in the spirit of Moses? Why not the spirit of Daniel? In an age of compromise and relativistic thinking, wouldn't the spirit of Daniel be effective? We could even argue for the spirit of David, Isaiah or Jeremiah, but why would John the Baptist go before the Lord in the spirit of Elijah?

Before I answer that question directly, let me set the context of this prophecy. The angel of the Lord came on the scene with this word after four hundred silent years. God had not spoken to anyone for four hundred years! The last words spoken by Him were in Malachi where He said He would send the prophet Elijah before the great and terrible day comes, and He would turn the hearts of the fathers to their children and the hearts of the children to their fathers. *(Malachi 4:5-6)* Then after four hundred years of silence, God sent the angel, Gabriel, to announce that John the Baptist would come and fulfill what was spoken four hundred years prior.

THE SPIRIT OF FATHERHOOD

So what does it mean for John the Baptist to come in the spirit of Elijah? To describe something as "the spirit of" is to describe the characteristics and distinctives of that particular object. If someone comes in the spirit of fear it means their demeanor is fearful and they act afraid. To say that John would come in the spirit of Elijah was to say that John would come displaying the characteristics of Elijah.

Though the Scriptures never give the exact description of the spirit of Elijah, I would submit to you that the spirit of Elijah is the spirit of fatherhood that seeks after the heart of a son. The spirit of Elijah is the spirit that seeks to build generationally. It is the spirit of a father who seeks for an Elisha and then gives himself fully to the transfer of all He is in God to that spiritual son. It is the same spirit that was operational in the relationship between Elijah and Elisha that resulted in Elisha crying out, *"My father! My father!"* (*II Kings 2:12*) when the whirlwind took Elijah to Heaven. The spirit that seeks to build generationally is nothing new. We can trace it all the way back to the Abrahamic covenant. Though God initiated the covenant with Abraham, He defined its borders to be *"an everlasting for all the generations to come."* (*Genesis 17:7*) In receiving that covenant, Abraham received a commission that not only claimed himself for God, but also claimed his descendants to come and the generations forevermore. Generational transfer was not an option for God. It was the only means employed for the covenant to be sustained throughout time. Generational transfer was not a suggestion for Abraham, it was a command.

"For I have chosen [Abraham], in order that he may command his children and his household after him to keep the way of the Lord..." (*Genesis 18:19 NAS*)

Abraham was chosen of God because God knew Abraham understood the necessity of generational transfer and in light of that necessity, would command his children, not merely make a suggestion to them.

So to receive the covenant is not only receiving a responsibility for ourselves, but we also receive an obligation to the multiple generations that will follow until Jesus comes.

BRIDGE GENERATION OR TERMINAL GENERATION

The truth of generational transfer is built upon the principle of being a bridge generation, not a terminal generation. Nearly every generation for the last one hundred years has said they are the terminal generation. That is, they thought they were the generation that would witness the *Second Coming* of the Lord. Consequently, they did very little to take dominion and had very little to pass on to the generations to come. The problem is the years have come and gone and we are still here on earth. In the mean time we have not occupied until Jesus comes, and as a result we have lost the territories of universities and business, the ruling of the nations, the arts, etc.

The church is not to live as a terminal generation; it is to live as a bridge generation, a generation between what was and what is to come. A bridge generation maintains a keen sense of responsibility both to the generations before and to the generations to come. It possesses both an historic accountability and a futuristic accountability. The worldview of a bridge generation sees truth coming to it and then passes it over to those who are to follow. Truth is never intended to stop with a generation. It comes to the generation, matures with the generation and is then passed on to the generation to follow. A bridge is something that joins two sides. Simply stated, a bridge generation exists to join the generation that was and the generation that is to come.

TITLE OR DESCRIPTION

Every time God identified Himself as the God of Abraham, Isaac and Jacob, He was not assigning Himself a title. He was giving Himself a description. The God of Abraham, Isaac and Jacob was not a title, but a description of His nature and His desire. His very nature is generational. He is past, present and future. And the generations past, present and future are inseparably fixed in His heart. It also describes His desire for us, in order to take on His nature and become like Him, we must live and think generationally.

We must live accountably to the past, relevant to the now and in anticipation of the future. This means we must live beyond ourselves. We must give our todays for our children's tomorrows. It is not enough that we just live under the blessing and make it to Heaven. We must not only fulfill our destiny, but we must equip our children to fulfill theirs.

IT'S A HEART ISSUE

The call to generational transfer is a call to the heart. The longer I am involved in discipleship and generational transfer, the more I am convinced the process is an issue of the heart. If the fathers are unwilling to give their hearts to their sons and the sons are unwilling to receive their father's hearts, the fruit of the process will never be realized. Please notice the focus of Malachi 4.6 was the hearts of the fathers and the hearts of the children. If the hearts of each were not for each other, God said He would "come and strike the land with a curse."

The curse of our day is *withheld hearts*. Some will give their money, give their time, even give to the point of sacrifice and yet all the time withhold the giving of their hearts. The focus of the fourth chapter of Malachi and the first chapter of Luke is on the heart. God is after our hearts, both the giving of our hearts and the receiving of another's heart. The only way the discipleship process can work is if the hearts of the disciple and the "discipler" are given to each other. Without hearts given to each other, discipleship can very easily become a means of control or manipulation. But when hearts are given to each other, the process is perceived as training. When hearts have not been given, the same process is often viewed as control.

It is here that we come to the very core of man's sin. *"We all, like sheep, have gone astray, each of us has turned to his own way." (Isaiah 53:6)* It is difficult to either give our heart to another or receive another's heart because our sin nature is bent on wanting its own way.

To carry the spirit of fatherhood is to exemplify a life laid down. To carry the spirit of sonship is to exemplify a life yielded to another. Both cut across the grain of independence and withheld hearts. Both deal a deathblow to that desire for our own way.

THE DOUBLE PORTION MINISTRY

I am convinced that it was prophesied that John would come in the spirit of Elijah because Elijah was the only prophet or anointed leader who passed on a double portion of his spirit to a son in the ministry. Elijah is the clearest example we have of a generational ministry. Yes, Abraham did it in the natural, but Elijah did it in the spirit. Both are vital and exemplify two facts of the generational call.

Elijah did not minister alone. He gave his heart to a son and Elisha was willing to receive the heart given. The giving and receiving resulted in a double portion ministry. God is desirous of double portion ministries today and He knows that we must seek to build the type of relationships Elijah and Elisha had. To do so will require the release of one person's heart and, subsequently, the willingness to receive that person's heart.

Many might say at this point that we are only to receive God's heart. They may think that to carry the heart of another man or woman is to encroach into God's sphere and usurp His authority. While this sounds noble and perhaps quite loyal, it is just not in harmony with the biblical record. The Scriptures are full of relationships that exemplify hearts given to one another.

Joshua certainly carried the heart of Moses. David and Jonathan were two whose hearts were entwined with each other. Paul had certainly given his heart to Timothy, and Timothy certainly carried Paul's heart. But perhaps the clearest example in Scripture is the example of Elijah and Elisha. Please note when given an opportunity to ask for anything from Elijah, Elisha asked for a double portion of Elijah's spirit, not God's.[1] It did not seem to bother God or Elijah that Elisha asked for a double portion of Elijah's spirit. When God granted Elisha his request he cried out, *"My father! My father!"* as Elijah was taken away. Again, God was not bothered by the fact that Elisha was calling another man to be his spiritual father.

The first quality a spiritual son should look for in a spiritual father is that he is wholly yielded and wholly sold out to God. To carry the heart of a spiritual father is to carry the heart of God, for the spiritual father's true heart is wholly united to Jesus.

ELIJAH'S GREATEST MIRACLE

What was Elijah's greatest miracle? Was it the three years of drought? Was it perhaps the calling down of fire? Or was it the showdown at Mount Carmel with the prophets of Baal? All of these miracles and the number of others were absolutely amazing. But I am convinced that Elisha's greatest miracle was with his son Elisha, for once Elijah was gone the double portion imparted to Elisha gave way for Elisha to do twice the miracles Elijah had done.

Whereas Elijah performed fourteen miracles, Elisha performed twenty-eight. It is amazing to note that many of those miracles performed by Elisha were exactly the same that Elijah had performed earlier. Both struck the water and it parted.[2] Both brought water in times of drought.[3] Both increased a widow's supply of food and oil.[4] Both called down vengeance on those against them.[5] But perhaps the greatest of these similarities was the raising of the sons from the dead. I Kings 17 gives the account of Elijah raising the boy from the dead. In verse 21 it says that Elijah stretched himself out on the boy three times and cried out to the Lord. The Lord heard Elijah's cry and on the third time the boy's life returned to him and he lived.

II Kings 4 gives the account of Elisha raising a boy from the dead. When Elisha had reached his parents' house, the boy was lying dead on the couch. Elisha went in with the boy and closed the door. He then prayed to the Lord. As he was praying he got on the couch and lay upon the boy, mouth to mouth, eyes to eyes, hands to hands. Elisha then got off the boy and walked around the room. He returned and stretched himself upon the boy a second time. While lying upon the boy a second time, the boy sneezed seven times and opened his eyes.

It is interesting to note that it took Elijah lying on the boy three times for him to be healed, but with the double portion anointing it took Elisha only twice. I am convinced with the double portion anointing the boy would have been healed with Elisha laying on him only one-and-a-half times. But how do you lay on someone half a time? Even after the first time from lying on the boy, he began to grow warm. The generational transfer from Elijah to Elisha meant greater and more intense miracles.

We can see in the similarities of these miracles that, even in the performing of miracles, Elisha was carrying the heart of his spiritual father, Elijah.

Donor and Recipient

The double portion blessing requires both donor and recipient. Fortunately for Elisha, he was not a twenty-first century American otherwise that independent spirit that so permeates our culture would have robbed him of his double portion blessing. Elijah was willing to be the donor and Elisha was willing to be the recipient.

"Elisha healed lepers, separated water from dry land and multiplied a few loaves of bread to feed a hundred men. He was so full of power that entire armies could not defeat him. Yet, he would have lived and died behind a plough, if Elijah had not given everything he had to the firstborn of his ministry."[6]

The spirit of Elijah is a heart given. The spirit of Elisha is a heart turned. The curse of our day is seen both in the inability to give one's heart and in the unwillingness to receive a heart that has been given.

The Church Has Lost Its Voice

Over the past one hundred years the church has consistently fallen from its stature of influence and prominence in society. Formerly standing at the top of the top of the most influencial institutions of the land, the church now ranks at the bottom. Nobody really cares anymore what the church thinks or about the morals it stands for. It used to be that society honored the meeting times of the church and did not schedule events for early Sunday morning or on Wednesday nights. But now, little concern is made for the church meeting times. Sports clubs schedule their times, filling both Sunday mornings and Wednesday evenings. The church has fallen from its significant stature in society and has lost its voice of influence.

Why has the church lost its voice and been so ineffective over the years? Could it be that we have not seen or believed in the importance of the spirit of Elijah? Look what happened to Zechariah when he did not receive Gabriel's word about John coming in the spirit of Elijah. Zechariah was struck silent for nine months until John was born.[7] Perhaps the silence of the church in regard to the reforming of society is due to the unwillingness of its sons to carry the hearts of its fathers and its fathers to impart their hearts to the sons.

A Return to Influence

Influence is lost when there is no generational transfer. Conversely, influence builds when there has been the transfer of truth throughout the generations. Four generations out from Abraham, we find Joseph administrating the affairs of a nation. Joseph's ability to administrate was inseparably linked to the faithfulness of Abraham, Isaac and Jacob to *"teach their children so the next generation would know them, even the children yet to be born."*[8] Each generation saw the increase of wealth and influence until the fourth generation saw Joseph raised up by God to a place of administration and powerful influence. Joseph still ruled a nation in spite of the injustice done to him by his brothers and in spite of his time in prison. Generational transfer equates to influence and influence happens regardless of man's attempt to obliterate it.

The Inheritance of the Heart

Jesus was the embodiment of carrying another's heart. Jesus did not come to promote His own way or exert His own heart. Receiving the inheritance of His Father's heart is an attribute of Jesus in which we are to share. There are communicable and non-communicable attributes of Jesus. The inheritance of Father's heart is a communicable one. It is the attribute of a heart received that breaks the spirit of independence in a man or woman, allowing him to receive the spirit of Elijah and reverse the curse on our land.

The American culture in particular has promoted the pride of origination. The pride of origination is that drive within man that elevates wanting to be original, to the most desired place. Americans in particular pride themselves on wanting to be original, but originality is not an attribute of the Kingdom of God. The Kingdom of God does not promote origination; it promotes succession. Jesus did not pride Himself on being original, but rather on carrying His Father's heart and doing nothing apart from Him. Sonship sees carrying a Father's heart as an honor; it is something to be encouraged, not disdained. In the Kingdom of God, our goal is not to be original, but to learn how to be a son.

The Frustration of Two Kings

"I have seen another evil under the sun, and it weighs heavily on men: God gives a man wealth, possessions and honor, so that he lacks nothing his heart desires, but God does not enable him to enjoy them, and a stranger enjoys them instead. This is meaningless, a grievous evil." (Ecclesiastes 6:1-2)

King David's frustration was that he saw something in the spirit, but he was not permitted to build it. King Solomon's frustration was that, though he was permitted to build what his father saw, and though he certainly had sons, none of them apperently qualified for his inheritance as none carried his heart. God had permitted Solomon to gather wealth, possessions and honor, but a stranger was to inherit it all for he as a father failed to give his heart to his sons.

The tragedy of this story is seen in the fact that King Solomon saw enough in the spirit to receive his father's heart, but he lacked what was needed to pass his heart on to his sons who followed him.

"The Lord has kept the promise He made: I have succeeded David my father..."
(I Kings 8:20)

Solomon defined success in terms of succession. He glowed in the fact that he was permitted to succeed his father. And though he was wise and prosperous, he never sought origination. In fact, he thanked God that he was permitted to succeed his father, not wanting to be original, but for some reason he never passed that spirit on to his sons.

"Again I saw something meaningless under the sun: There was a man all alone; he had neither son nor brother. There was no end to his toil, yet his eyes were not content with his wealth. 'For whom am I toiling,' he asked, 'and why am I depriving myself of enjoyment?' This too is meaningless—a miserable business! Two are better than one, because they have a good return for their work: If one falls down, his friend can help him up. But pity the man who falls and has no one to help him up! Also, if two lie down together, they will keep warm. But how can one keep warm alone? Though one may be overpowered, two can defend themselves. A cord of three strands is not quickly broken."(Ecclesiastes 4:7-12)

I have always struggled a bit with the book of Ecclesiastes because it seemed so pessimistic. But now I am beginning to see some insight into the "meaningless" of which Solomon wrote.

We can see from the above passage that Solomon saw the need of someone to carry his heart, though for some reason, he never chose to pass it on, or was it that his sons never chose to receive it. Consequently, he concluded that all else was meaningless, as there was no one to inherit his heart.

Life is ultimately meaningless without our receiving and carrying the heart of God. It is equally meaningless if we fail to receive the heart of another and neglect the passing of our hearts to those who follow us.

Life in the Kingdom of God is found in succession, which has a two step process:

> Receiving the heart of a father.
> Passing your heart on to a son.

The passion of Jesus was expressed in the desire to receive the heart of His Father and then pass His heart on to us. The essence of sonship is expressed in the ability to receive, carry and impart Father's heart to all those we come in contact with.

"And he will go on before the Lord, in the spirit and power of Elijah, to turn the hearts of the fathers to their children and the disobedient to the wisdom of the righteous—to make ready a people prepared for the Lord." (Luke 1:17)

To be a people prepared for the Lord is to be a people with turned hearts:

> Hearts turned to God.

> Hearts turned to fathers.

> Hearts turned to sons.

If you are stuck in the pride of origination or find yourself a prisoner to the spirit of independence, I encourage you right now to repent and turn your way over to God. Allow Him to replace that spirit of independence with the spirit of Elijah.

FOOTNOTES:

1. II Kings 2:9
2. II Kings 2:8; 2:14
3. I Kings 18:41; II Kings 3:20
4. I Kings 17:5; II Kings 4:1
5. II Kings 1:10; 2:23
6. *You have not Many Fathers*, Dr. Mark Hanby, Destiny Image, p.63
7. Luke 1:20
8. Psalm 78:5-6

The ANCIENT PATH of
GENERATIONAL TRANSFER

WHEN IT CAME TO DEFINING HIMSELF, Jesus gave us this description. He said, *"I am the way..."(John 14:6)* Jesus is not just the embodiment of truth; He is also the way in which that truth is walked out. The result of modernity in the church has been an end justifies the means rationale. Because Jesus is the way, however, the means is equally as important as the end.

LIVING MODERN

For years Rocky Balboa captivated the hearts and dreams of countless viewers in theaters across America. His underdog determination and commitment to pay the price inspired the hearts of all. The problem was success came with a price. Once Rocky began to taste the sweet life, he started to forget who he was and what it was that took him to the top. The Vegas hotel soon replaced the ghetto gym. The glitter and the glitz replaced the hard strenuous workouts. The *eye of the tiger* was replaced with the look of complacency. Consequently, when Rocky stepped into the ring with Clubber Lang, he was not the same man who had defeated Apollo Creed and the opponents that followed. Complacency led to Rocky's defeat.

Disappointed by his defeat Rocky turned to his former opponent for help. He asked Apollo Creed to assume the role of trainer and asked him to train him for a rematch with Clubber Lang. Upon acceptance of the invitation, Apollo Creed made a watershed evaluation. Remembering how Rocky once trained and seeing the glitz of his current method, Apollo said, "Rocky you've been living modern, and now it's time to train old." The next scene found Rocky back in the ghetto gym, once again to have climbed to being the notorious eye of the tiger.

Similarly, the church has been living modern. The ways of modernity have replaced the ancient paths of generational transfer. The one on one relationship of mentor and disciple has been replaced with one impersonal instructor and a classroom of a hundred students. A lifetime of *formation* has been replaced with a few short years of *information*. The church has been living modern, but it is time to train old.

"This is what the Lord says, 'Stand at the crossroads and look; ask for the ancient paths, ask where the good way is, and walk in it, and you will find rest for your souls.'" (Jeremiah 6:16)

Standing at the Crossroads

The church today stands at the crossroads of decision. The decision is whether to train its members according to modern thought or to ask for the ancient path. Modern thought tells us that children must decide for themselves. Modern thought tells us the authority roll of parents is abusive. Modern thought tells us yesterday's values cannot be applied to today's children. Modern thought is in us more than we care to admit. Its power is subtle, but its result is comprehensive.

The church has been living modern, but it is time to train old. A vision for generational transfer is a vision to return to the ancient path. Modern thought is the way of information without transformation. Modern thought allows an instructor to simply be the dispenser of information without pressing the students for transformation. Yes, it is only the Holy Spirit who can transform, but an instructor on the ancient path will hold transformation up as the standard and not be satisfied when the students settle for information only.

Transformation vs. Symptom Management

Modern thought focuses on the managing of symptoms as opposed to transformation. The philosophies of this world system have turned symptom management into an art form. People have become masters at managing their problems rather than pressing for their elimination.

I was recently told a classic illustration of the futility of trying to manage what needs to be eliminated. A judge ordered a man into an anger management course. The first night the man attended, he disrupted the class so badly he was asked by the instructor to leave. He returned a second time and again disrupted the class so was asked by the instructor to leave. He returned a third time and his disruption became so disturbing that the instructor of the anger management class, escorted the man outside into the parking lot and within window view of his class, beat the man to death. This is the result of information without transformation.

The best that modern thought can offer us is management. But it is nothing short of cruelty to instruct someone to manage his sin when the Bible instructs us how to put that sin to death.

The ancient path is the way of transformation through impartation. On the ancient path you find Moms and Dads who transform the lives of their children because they take the time to impart to them the truth they have found in Christ. On the ancient path you find pastors and mentors who sow a vision for transformation into the generation to come. These will not be the ones who will settle for simple instruction. They will instruct and then be an example, emulating that what they taught— thus making a way for transformation.

The Way Redefined

Modern thought defines success in terms of origination. Modern thought tells us a successful person is an original person. Modern thought is driven by a carnal need to be original. This need to be original is nothing more than radical independence dressed up in a more user-friendly title.

Jesus Christ was the least original man who ever walked the earth. Without apology He said, *"The Son can do nothing by himself; he can do only what he sees his father doing." (John 5:19)* It is not that He was not capable of original thought. He had no carnal need to be original. He was perfectly content in bearing the image and likeness of His Father.

A man once said to me, "I will never be a Christian because they are all clones." I said to him, "You are exactly right." The fact of the matter is we are all clones of someone or something, for there is nothing new under the sun. While the man was giving me his clone defense, I did happen to notice his Nike tennis shoes, Calvin Klein jeans and Tommy Hilfelger shirt. Though he prided himself on his origination, there were about three million others who were exactly as original as he was!

Origination of Succession

The ancient path defines success, not in terms of origination, but in terms of succession. To succeed on the ancient path is to abide faithfully in what has been imparted to men and then reproduce in others the life of Christ that has been deposited in you. Success on the ancient path is not an issue of origination, but one of reproduction.
"Moses my servant is dead. Now then, you..." (Joshua 1:1)

The key to Joshua's success was not finding some new way that was different from Moses' way. The issue for Joshua was not the superiority of his way over the way of Moses. Joshua's responsibility was to remain in the way God had established through Moses, without succumbing to the carnal need to establish his own way of proving himself.

Often I hear parents and children who say that at eighteen you must go out and find your own way. The underlying shame behind that philosophy is the former way they were following, namely their parents' way, was wrong. If their parents' way were right there would be no need to find an alternative way. As parents with a vision of generational transfer, we must not fall into this deception of modernity. The way for our children to follow, whether they are eighteen or eighty-four, is the way of the Kingdom of God. To the degree that we are walking in that Kingdom, we must raise our children with a vision to succeed us and not be pressured into a carnal need to "find their own way." Their way must be our way, and our way must be the ancient way of the Kingdom of God.

We must raise our children and those coming up behind us with an expectation of succession. Everyone of them will face the day as did Joshua when he or she will hear the words, "Now then, you." How they will receive that commission will be determined by how deep we have laid the seed of expectation and trained the next generations in the joy of responsibility.

King Solomon carried this expectation of succession. The Lord had put it in the heart of Solomon's father, David, to build a temple. Though David carried that in his heart, he was not permitted by the Lord to build it. The sovereignty of God had ordained that one generation would formulate the vision and the next generation would fulfill it.

"Because it was in your heart to build a temple for my Name, you did well to have this in your heart. Nevertheless, you are not the one to build the temple, but your son, who is your own flesh and blood—he is the one who will build the temple for my Name." (I Kings 8:18-19)

The will of God was clearly spoken. David was a man of war, so he was not the one to fulfill the dream; he was just the one to conceive it. Many dreams are lost because they were never passed to the second generation. Dreams of an eternal nature are conceived by one generation and built by another. It is the responsibility of the dream *conceivers* to sow their dream into the hearts of *builders* in the next generation. If the dream conceivers are unable to pass on their dream, the generation that is designed to build it will only be dream conceivers rather than dream builders.

Destiny is a cycle of conceiving and building. One generation conceives; the next generation builds. The builders must receive the dream from the conceivers lest they **seek to conceive when they have been ordained of God to build. "The Lord has kept the promise He made: I have succeeded David my father..."** (I Kings 8:20)

Solomon defined success in terms of succession, not origination. He did not ask the Lord for his own dream. He did not desire to be a dream conceiver. He saw that his destiny was to succeed his father and be a dream builder.

How many frustrated ministries do we have in Christendom today because they are either trying to build when they were only to conceive, or they are trying to conceive when they were ordained to build? Yes, the sovereignty of God can ordain for one generation to do both, but usually the Lord chooses one generation to conceive it and another generation to build it. Our responsibility is to discern our position before God and not presume we are to just conceive, just build or even do both. We are to do only what He has ordained for us to do which includes preparing the coming generation for what remains.

Spiritual Compound Interest

The church as a whole has been robbed of the power inherent in successive generations. Nearly every generation has started over. Consequently, we have never been able to establish the power of momentum or experience the spiritual application of compound interest.

Compound interest in the banking world is simply the reality where the investment starts multiplying from itself. Even a small investment subjected to compound interest, will become large, given enough time. The church has certainly had the time necessary. Unfortunately, we have been living modern and not investing in the coming generation. Consequently, we do not possess the power and influence of "old money."

Having traveled through Europe, I have come to appreciate the value of "old money." Old money is simply money that has been passed down through the generations. With the value of land being high as it is in most of Europe, young families could never own a home out-right or some other kind of property without it being passed down to them. Through inheritance, the worth and value of the previous generation becomes theirs at which point they have the opportunity to build upon that foundation. Then their children and their children's children can succeed, doing the same for their children to follow.

Such is the vision of generational transfer. Through spiritual inheritance our physical and spiritual children can receive a running start from us. They can catch the baton at full speed and run the remainder of the race to win.

A RUNNING START

Canadian runner, Donovan Bailey, won the 1996, 100-meter gold medal with a speed of 9.84 seconds. Though Donovan won the gold medal, his 9.84 seconds was not the fastest 100-meter race run in the '96 Olympics. The fact is there were many who ran but did not win gold. A faster 100 meter race was actually run by every runner of the 100 meter relay who succeeded him in the 2nd, 3rd, and 4th positions. The reason was, when they received the baton at their starting line, they had the privilege of starting at a full sprint. Consequently, they were able to run the entire race at full speed without having to begin at a dead stop. The momentum was already established as the baton was placed in their hands.

A vision for generational transfer is a vision to see our children begin with a running start. We all begin as first generation believers, as God has no grandchildren. He only has sons and daughters. But each generation must get a running start in reference to the vision, blessings, ministry and effectiveness that will reach into the 2nd generation, the 3rd, and the generations beyond. These are the Isaac and the Jacob generations, where the ground, gained by the fathers who have gone before, is not lost. These are the generations that receive double and triple blessings. They inherit all that their forefathers received plus all that God imparts to them directly.

A PERSONAL TESTIMONY

Such has been the case in our lives. My wife and I were recipients of a running start, though Marcy and I are first generation believers. But we are 2nd

Am I willing to sacrifice and make commitment to invest into my kids?

generation ministers. By virtue of having been discipled by those who have gone before us, we have received a double blessing. When we started Christ Church Kirkland in 1985, we had the privilege of beginning with a running start. Pastor Jim Hamann who commissioned us and sent us out had already laid a foundation that provided for an incredible inheritance.

As a young congregation, we already understood worship. We understood the importance of spiritual authority. The seed of the Kingdom of God had already been sown. People came on Sunday with Bibles and notebooks, ready to worship and ready to learn. This was an inheritance from the generation before us.

When that inevitable day will come to those who follow me and they hear the commissioning words of *"Now then, you. . ."* they will begin with a triple blessing. They will be the Jacob generation that inherits all that was Abraham's, all that was Isaac's, and that which God gives uniquely to them. We will be forever grateful for that which Pastor Jim and others have sown into our lives, for it has enabled us to build upon the concept of "old money."

"O my people, hear my teaching; listen to the words of my mouth. I will open my mouth in parables, I will utter hidden things, things from of old what we have heard and known, what our fathers have told us. We will not hide them from their children; we will tell the next generation the praiseworthy deeds of the Lord, his power, and the wonders He has done. He decreed statutes for Jacob and established the law in Israel, which he commanded our forefathers to teach their children, so the next generation would know them, even the children yet to be born, and they in turn would tell their children. Then they would put their trust in God and would not forget His deeds but would keep His commands."
(Psalm 78:1-7)

The ancient path is a progressive journey designed to be built generation upon generation with the present generation taking the purposes of God further than the former. We see in verses 5 and 6, God's command to Israel covered a span of three to four generations. In reality it covers a span of all time that becomes a complex web of safety and transformation. The three generations secure my position in the race, defining my part in the eternal responsibility I have for the next generation.

A Complex Web of Safety

When each generation recognizes and embraces its responsibility for passing the baton on to the 2nd and 3rd generations to follow, a complex web of safety and transformation is formed. When the 1st generation embraces this, the responsibility is grasped tightly, with each generation receiving discipling and care from two other generations.

When I assume responsibility to disciple my son and grandson, my grandson will be receiving the way of the ancient path both from me and my son, his own father. Consequently, he receives double coverage. Where there is generational transfer, each generation realizes a multiplication effect. The calling upon Abraham produced one son of promise. The calling upon Isaac produced two. But the calling upon Jacob produced twelve sons of promise.

With each successive generation the credibility of Christianity is strengthened and the influence of its testimony is broadened. The church has all but lost its influence in the world because we do not have the successive generations to authenticate the power and authenticity of our message. Society is looking for the authentic. They have seen religion and were not impressed. They have tasted the insincere and were not satisfied. Now they long for the authentic and cry out for the true sons to be revealed. This level of authenticity is found only in the succession of the generations.

> First Generation — Fathers Formulate
> Second Generation — Sons Demonstrate
> Third Generation — Sons Authenticate

Without a vision for generational transfer the church is forever in the formation stage. To impact society and be the city on a hill that the Word of God says we are, we must progress to the stages of demonstration and authentication.

This world has become quite pragmatic. People are more concerned with whether something works than they are with what it is. We have preoccupied ourselves with letting people know what Christianity is rather than demonstrating to them that it works. As we turn our focus to the way of generational transfer, we will find that what comes with the 2nd and 3rd generations will speak for itself. In the 2nd and 3rd generation, our saltiness will be restored and our influence will once again be established.

How Does Generational Transfer Take Place?

1. It starts with a vision.

"Where there is no revelation the people cast off restraint..." (*Proverbs 29:18*) Possession always begins with a seed of expectation. Long before something is actually possessed, it is first seen through the eyes of the spirit. Vision is something the Holy Spirit allows us to see concerning the purposes and intent of God, seeing with His eyes the future and plans He has for us.

Without a vision for generational transfer we will cast off the restraint necessary to accomplish it. A vision for generational transfer begins by realizing that our children and those God brings into our lives are His. They have been given to us, not as a possession, but as a stewardship. As in the stewardship of anything God gives us, we must show a profit on His investment. This is done by imparting to them a vision of the Kingdom of God and showing them how they fit into it.

We must give our children a vision for something bigger than themselves. God has designed youth to be full of zeal and ambitious desire. Their ideals are high and their intentions big. We must present to them a vision that will capture those ideals and channel that zeal. Often in fear of being too hard on them, we water down the expectations and compromise the price. Consequently, they are not challenged and their ideals are not hired. A vision that is only self-serving will never capture the youth. We must give them a vision to change the world and be a part of an eternal army that will rule and subdue the earth as commissioned by God in the dominion mandate.[13]

Parents and leaders today are afraid to lead. Perhaps in fear of being controlling, they leave those in their care to fend for themselves. Without leadership and someone to draw destiny out of our youth, very few will ever fulfill their calling.

The calling on Abraham's life to become a great and powerful nation through which all the nations on earth would be blessed was immense. But Abraham's calling was not his alone. His calling had to be imparted to his son and to his son's son in order for the desire of God to be fulfilled. Wishful thinking was not enough to ensure Abraham's success. It had to be more purposeful than that. God had to ensure that Abraham would take leadership and direct the lives of his children into the way they should go.

"For I have chosen [Abraham] so that he will direct his children and his household after him to keep the way of the Lord by doing what is right and just, so that the Lord will bring about for Abraham what He has promised him." (Genesis 18:19)

This word "direct" comes with it authority and expectation. It is not direction by suggestion, but direction by command. It involves aggressive leadership. When we recognize the seriousness of the call, we know it demands a magnitude of direction. It means we must pray and ask God to show us who our children are. Once we see them through His eyes, we are on safe ground to begin our directing.

2. We must spend time with our youth.

Discipleship is the means of generational transfer. The transfer takes place little by little over a long period of time. A recent study showed the average father spends an average of seventeen seconds a day with his children. Seventeen seconds a day will indeed give a generational transfer, but the transfer will not be what we desire it to be.

Generational transfer is the way of impartation through emulation. To impart requires time. For our youth to emulate us they must be with us enough to see how we respond in adversity, how we relate to God in every day life.

PRACTICAL SUGGESTIONS FOR FATHERS

Fathers, understand the importance of time spent with your children. Do not *send* your children to bed at night, *put* them to bed.

"These commandments that I give you today are to be upon your hearts. Impress them on your children. Talk about them when you sit at home and when you walk along the road, when you lie down and when you get up." (Deuteronomy 6:6-7)

Putting your children to bed at night with the Word, prayer and conversation is an excellent opportunity to spend time with them. It gives fathers a chance to individually sit with them and filter through their day. Anything that was picked up throughout the day that is contrary to the Kingdom way can be disposed of and replaced with the truth. We can speak to them concerning their destiny and tell them who they are in the Lord. We can interpret their dreams and desires by the measure of God's Word and make adjustments where necessary. We can pray over them and prophesy to them and, in so doing impart Father's heart to them.

Putting my children to bed at night has been one of the highlights of my life. I love just being there with them, giving them my undivided attention. Along with that, our children need time alone with Dad on a regular basis that is their time that they can count on as their special time. Every week, one of my children and I have a breakfast together, just the two of us. Every Monday morning for the past eleven years I've shared that unique time with my daughter, Kelsey. To date, that's over 1,000 breakfasts where we've had opportunity to talk, pray and plan, receiving God's destiny for her. Tuesday has been Kaleb's morning and Wednesday belongs to Kyle. As long as I am not traveling, they know this time is theirs.

 Value is defined in terms of time spent. To place value on children is to spend quality, undivided time with them. By doing so they are able to interpret our actions as tangible feelings of worth. If our pursuit of career, recreation or any other activity crowds out our children's time with us, they will learn to resent us and the values we stand for.

3. Draw your children into family purpose and ministry.

Purpose is not something limited to certain individuals. Not only does every individual have a God-given purpose, but also each family has a unique purpose before God Even as each individual in that family carries a unique God-given design, when those uniquenesses are put together in a family unit, it results in a unique family purpose.

Parents must pray and discern to determine what that purpose is. Perhaps it will be expressed in hospitality or in intercession. Maybe it will be found in outreach to the homeless or to neighborhood children. Whatever the calling, we must draw our children into it so they are able to experience the joy of being used by God. I am convinced that, if my children experience the wonder of being used of the Lord, they will never stray from Him. Many youth walk away from their roots because they see no relevance or sense of adventure in them. The Spirit-led walk is the most exciting adventure in life. The exhilaration that comes in being used of the Lord can be compared to nothing.

When my daughter was in high school, she had the privilege of travelling to Costa Rica with over thirty from her youth group. While there, she was given the opportunity to reach a potential audience of three million people while speaking on Costa Rican national radio. Kelsey returned from that impacting adventure with a life changing testimony of being used by the Lord. With plenty of those types of adventures to come, she won't be straying from the Lord in hopes of fulfilling her adventure needs.

When I was in high school, I got deeply involved in the drug scene. In retrospect, I now realize I was in search of the supernatural. God created us with a need to experience His supernatural life. If that need is not met in a relationship with Him, we might seek to fulfill it in some immoral or illegal way. As we draw our children into their family's purpose, their need for the supernatural will be met and the temptation to stray will be drastically lessened.

The key to children participating in their family's purpose is accomplished through our leading them into a personal and vital relationship with Christ. We must train them to spend time with the Lord daily. We must train them in early rising, Scripture reading, prayer and waiting on the Lord. For most, this does not come naturally. We must lead them by our example and by helping them manage their time so that they can learn to do this.

Another way to draw them into the family purpose is to teach them how to tie all material and spiritual blessing directly to our relationship to the Lord and His favor on the family.

Our ministry has opened the door for us to minister to many professional athletes. We have been invited to Pro Bowls with football players and have had players into our home on many occasions. My son has been given autographed team balls, autographed Pro Bowl balls and many other sports memorabilia.

Our family has been invited to Europe and Africa, as well as many places within the United States. With each invitation and every blessing, we make sure our children understand that it has all come about for one reason and one reason only—the ministry of the Lord Mom and Dad carry. If it were not for who we are in the Lord and the doors Father has opened for us, we would have none of these adventures.

As our children learn to tie these blessings back to the Lord and His purpose for our lives, they begin to see the joy and blessing it is to serve the Lord. This helps balance out what is possibly perceived as their loss when Mom and Dad are gone or when they seem preoccupied It also helps them to see that serving the Lord is fun. All too often adults speak negatively of the church in the home. As the children hear those negative words, they conclude that ministry and perhaps even Christianity is not for them. After all, "If Mom and Dad are this negative about it, why would I want to follow?"

A RETURN TO THE ANCIENT PATH

Generational transfer is a hot topic in Christian circles today, but be assured; this is not just another "flavor of the month" topic. It is being spoken of in many circles because the Holy Spirit is bringing it to the forefront. Generational transfer is not a new topic. It is as old as God's commission to man. From the beginning His plan of succession has been through the generations.

"He decreed statutes for Jacob and established the law in Israel, which He commanded our forefathers to teach their children, so the next generation would know them, even the children yet to be born, and they in turn would tell their children." (Psalm 78:5-6)

Let this be a call to you to return to the ancient pathway of generational transfer. Let it be a call to give up your todays in order to establish your children's tomorrows.

The THREE PHASES of
GENERATIONAL TRANSFER

how get to next level of responsibility?
• Disciple someone—

responsible for yourself— actions.

GENERATIONAL TRANSFER DOES NOT JUST HAPPEN. It occurs as the result of strategic planning and purposeful living. Because God is a God of order and design, He follows a definite order to transfer the truth from generation to generation.

The transfer of truth as it comes to man is both linear and progressive in its nature. Truth comes to us in seed form and then unfolds progressively over time. Such is the case in generational transfer. Generational transfer does not just happen overnight. The transfer of truth is accomplished in phases and with each phase consisting of various stages.

The intent of this chapter is to describe three phases of generational transfer and four stages of spiritual growth within those three phases.

PHASE I	PHASE II	PHASE III
CHILDHOOD	SONSHIP	FATHERHOOD
STAGE I: RESPONSBILITY	STAGE II: APPRENTICESHIP	STAGE III: STEWARDSHIP
I'LL DO, YOU WATCH	YOU DO, I'LL WATCH	YOU DO FOR ANOTHER

JESUS THE PATTERN SON

"For unto us a child is born, to us a Son is given...and He will be called Everlasting Father." (Isaiah 9:6)

Though He was the incarnate Son of God, Jesus was not born in the fullness of stature. Jesus was not born complete in His capacity to obey. *"Although he was a son, he learned obedience from what He suffered." (Hebrews 5:8)* Being the pattern Son, Jesus was subjected to the same progressive timetable that we are. Though He was God, He was brought through the same phases of transfer. Now we must embrace these same stages of growth. Jesus was born a child, matured to a Son and ultimately became the Everlasting Father.

In the three phases we see the pattern of generational transfer that all must go through. As we embrace them and the corresponding stages of growth with each, we prepare the way by example for the generations that are coming after us.

PHASE I: CHILDHOOD

"I write to you dear children..." (1 John 2:12) Childhood is a beautiful phase of life. By its very nature it is designed by God to be a time of growth and development. We come into childhood knowing nothing and every day is a new lesson full of new information and new challenge. Jesus understood this beginning phase of generational transfer and made it the prerequisite to entering into the Kingdom of God. He said, *"...Unless you change and become like little children, you will never enter the Kingdom of Heaven." (Matthew 18:3)* To be childlike is quite different from acting childish. Regardless of our age in the natural, we must assume childlike qualities in order to enter the Kingdom of Heaven.

CHILDLIKE QUALITIES

rest in God

I. The simple trust of being cared for and the security it brings.

As children grow they have no cause for worry. From the time they are born until the time they reach maturity, many children have all their needs cared for. They never worry whether they will have a house to live in. They never worry whether they will have clothes to wear. They never worry whether there will be food for the next meal. For the most part, their early years are carefree, for they have learned to place their trust in the provisional ability of their parents. The ability of their parents to provide both their natural and spiritual needs instills into them a confidence and a security.

Father brings us into the Kingdom of God as children because He wants to teach us to trust Him. He brings us in as children so we can experience firsthand the provisional ability of our heavenly Father. He tells us to consider how the lilies grow, they do not labor or spin. And if that is how He cares for them, how much more will He care for us *(Matthew 6.48)*?

Childhood is that phase in our life when we learn the simple trust in Father's provisional care. If we skip the childhood phase, and therefore our sonship, and are thrust immediately into the challenges of adulthood, we will have an inadequate foundation of trust to meet those challenges.

2. The unconditional nature of Father's love.

As children grow, they learn they cannot earn their parent's love or behave in a manner where they try to deserve it. For the first couple of years of life, children are totally unable to give productively to the family. The initial stages of their life consist of eating, sleeping and having messy diapers, yet the parents are totally in love with them. Though they wake the parents in the middle of the night and spit up on the freshly cleaned clothes, they are still loved. As they grow they have the unique ability to destroy the home and break cherished keepsakes, yet the parents still love them.

How is this possible? It is the nature of unconditional love. Unconditional love by its very nature says, "You cannot earn my love or perform in such a way as to deserve it." Unconditional love loves in spite of, not because of. *good*

Childhood is that phase in our life when we learn the unconditional nature of Father's love, when we can only receive. We could never qualify for Father's love; we need only to accept it. When we come to Him as children, we learn He does not want our performance. He only wants our faith and belief. As children, we learn that grace really does work.

3. Correction is not rejection.

"And you have forgotten that word of encouragement that addresses you as sons: 'My son, do not make light of the Lord's discipline, and do not lose heart when He rebukes you, because the Lord disciplines those He loves, and He punishes everyone He accepts as a son." (Hebrews 12:5-6)

Sonship is not the absence of discipline, but the willful embracing of it. The writer of Hebrews exhorts us to see that the love of God is demonstrated by His willingness to discipline and correct those He loves.

In God's economy, correction is a sign of love, not rejection. To ignore the need to correct your children is a sign of your rejection of them. David understood this truth when he said, *"Let a righteous man strike me—it is a kindness; let him rebuke me—it is oil on my head. My head will not refuse it ..."* (Psalm 141:5) David welcomed correction as a kindness as he realized the need for change. He saw someone's willingness to correct him as a sign of his love and affection, not a form of rejection.

As children grow within the love and security of a family, they learn the necessity of correction and do not associate it with rejection. They grow up learning that correction is a normal part of the growing process, provided it is done in love with a vein toward maturity. Such is the case in the Kingdom of God. Correction, whether it be from our heavenly Father or from a spiritual father, is a kindness, not a form of rejection.

4. Failure is a necessary step in the process of maturity.

Failure cannot be separated from childhood. As they learn to walk, children fail in their first steps. Learning to talk, they fail in their first words. Most of their initial attempts are marked by failure. As spiritual children, we too must learn that failure is a necessary step in the journey toward maturity.

Failure does not disqualify what God has pre-qualified. Our pre-qualification in God is predicated upon the finished work of Christ, not upon our ability to perform without mistakes.

"Though a righteous man falls seven times, he rises again..." (*Proverbs 24:16*) Please note that it is the *righteous* man who falls seven times, not the unrighteous. Failing is such a necessary part of our journey into maturity that even those who walk in righteousness still stumble and experience failure.

Toys-R-Us Christians

There is nothing wrong with the phase of childhood provided you do not stay there. Childhood is a necessary and essential phase in our journey toward maturity, but it is not a destination. There are those who refuse to grow up, still wanting the toys of childhood. Though forty years old, many are still children when they should be fathers.

Moving through the stages of childhood and sonship to fatherhood requires purposeful and intentional living. One must act deliberately in life to progress through the phases of maturity and the various stages of each.

Paul stated it this way, *"When I was a child, I talked like a child, I reasoned like a child. When I became a man, I put childish ways behind me."* (*I Corinthians 13:11*) Childish ways are not necessarily sinful ways. They are past ways that are appropriate only to children. We all reach the time in our lives when it is time to decidedly lay aside our childish ways and embrace the maturity of sonship. It is here that childish habits of irresponsibility are laid aside and we adopt the posture of responsible living.

Stage One: Responsibility; I'll do; you watch

Phase I, (Childhood), is a time of spiritual growth that we all enter. Childhood begins irresponsibly, but ends with much responsibility. As parents who believe in the necessity of generational transfer, we must strive to instill within our children a sense of responsibility.

Childhood is that phase in our lives where we are trained to embrace incremental levels of responsibility that prepare us for the function of sonship and fatherhood. *"And if you have not been trustworthy with someone else's property, who will give you property of your own?" (Luke 16:12)*

To come into the fullness of sonship we must learn the responsibility of serving and caring for what does not belong to us. We learn the responsibility of serving another man's vision even as Elisha served Elijah and Timothy served Paul.

It is interesting to note that Adam already had a job before he was given a woman *(Genesis 2.20)*. Before Adam was given the pleasure of a woman at his side, he was given the responsibility of naming the animals. In the Kingdom of God, duty comes before honor, responsibility before pleasure.

Generational transfer is the understanding that God has put the future of His family into our hands. The essence of leadership is learning how to embrace the responsibility of stewardship of both the future and the past. There is a historic continuity that we must be responsible for and a future continuity that we must equip our children to be responsible to.

Responsibility is understood in recognizing representation. No generation is self-appointed. Every generation serves under a represented authority. That is, we do not represent ourselves; we represent Jesus Christ and His Kingdom purposes in this life. Without the embracing of responsibility our representation will be misrepresentation.

Often people ask, "What is the most important thing I can do to become a leader?" My answer to that question is, "Embrace responsibility." Responsibility will take us to deeper levels of intimacy with Jesus and higher levels of effectiveness in His Kingdom. Responsibility will enable us to say *yes* when all from within us cries out *no*.

I wish I could say I have done what I have done out of my pure love and devotion to Jesus, but the reality is, much of what I have done has been due to my sense of responsibility, not devotion. My goal is devotion, but until that devotion becomes my sole motivation, I will allow responsibility to motivate me and keep me in Kingdom pursuit.

Responsibility is what instills into our children a vision compelling enough to restrain them from stealing from their future. Responsibility is what instills in parents a vision compelling enough to redeem their past. *"Moses my servant is dead. Now then, you..." (Joshua 1:2)*

Every twenty years or so a spiritual family faces the parting of a generation. It is during this time, as it was with Joshua, that the mantle of leadership passes from the father to the son. The success of that transfer is predicated upon the level of responsibility in which the son has been equipped to walk.

Responsibility is the stage where the fathers say, "I'll do; you watch." Joshua spent forty years watching Moses and being trained under his righteous influence. Can you imagine the weight of responsibility that fell on Joshua's shoulders when he heard those words, *"Now then you"?* In spite of the weight Joshua rose to the challenge and embraced his responsibility.

There will likewise come a day when our sons and daughters will hear the words, *"Now then, you..."* Consequently, we must train them today to embrace the responsibility necessary to realize their tomorrows. We must live lives worthy of emulation, knowing at all times they are watching us and will emulate what they see.

PHASE II: SONSHIP

"And a voice came from heaven: 'You are my Son, whom I love; with you I am well pleased.'" (Mark 1:11)

This statement from Father was not a reiteration of Christ's identity, but a declaration of His qualification. Father was declaring to Jesus and to the principalities and powers of the unseen world that the "child born" had become the "son given." Sonship for Jesus was an action not a position. Jesus demonstrated His sonship by His willingness to yield Himself fully to Father's eternal plan. He did not consider His equality with God as something to be grasped. Rather, He yielded Himself and demonstrated what He was in position through action.

We are all sons of God by position. *"The Spirit Himself testifies with our spirit that we are God's children." (Romans 8:16)* If the Spirit of God resides in us, we are sons of God. But who we are by position is often quite different from who we are by behavior. Paul makes a behavioral distinction of sonship as well *"...because those who are led by the Spirit are sons of God." (Romans 8:14)* Sonship is both a position and a behavior. It is both a noun and a verb. On one hand it describes who I am and, on the other hand, it describes what I do.

Positional sonship is automatic with rebirth. If I am born again I am a son of God. Behavioral sonship is predicated upon one behaving as a son. To be a son by behavior, I must allow the Spirit of God to lead me. You can be a church member and never become a son in behavior. Positional sonship is automatic, but behavioral sonship is revelational.

THE SPIRIT OF SONSHIP

Sonship is not a teaching. It is a spirit. *"For you did not receive a spirit that makes you a slave again to fear, but you received the spirit of sonship." (Romans 8:15)* Since sonship is a spirit, sonship becomes a way. If we say someone has a spirit of fear, we are saying they consistently act fearful. Fear has become a way of life for them. They act fearful in all they do. Likewise, to have the spirit of sonship operational in our lives means that we act as sons in all we do. Sonship becomes an attitude that affects every aspect of our behavior.

Sonship is like a pair of glasses. If our glasses are colored, everything we see takes on the same color. Once sonship is operational in our behavior it affects everything we see and do. If sonship is not working in our lives, then every other *ship* goes astray. Without a clear understanding of sonship, worship becomes performance, discipleship becomes duty, stewardship becomes possessive, fellowship becomes exclusive, and so on. Sonship keeps our focus properly aligned and doing it keeps other *ships* on the proper course.

The spirit of sonship affects both what we are and what we do. The spirit of sonship addresses both the general aspects of our lives and the specific ones. Generally speaking, we are all sons of God. Consequently, we interact with all of life from the perspective of sonship. Specifically, we must also become sons of the one the sovereignty of God has joined us to *(II Corinthians 12.18; Ephesians 4.16)*. We must become sons of the house, and sons of the vision.

Such was the case with Elisha and Elijah. As Elijah was being carried up to Heaven in a whirlwind, Elisha cried out, *"My father! My father!" (II Kings 2:12)* Elijah was not the natural father of Elisha. Their relationship was one of spiritual birth. Elisha had become a spiritually born son of Elijah. The spirit of sonship was operational in their relationship. Consequently, Elisha received a double portion of his father's spirit. Generational transfer was evident.

The relationship of Paul and Timothy is another example of the spirit of sonship being operational in two people's lives.

"Even though you have ten thousand guardians in Christ, you do not have many fathers, for in Christ Jesus I became your father through the Gospel. Therefore I urge you to imitate me. For this reason I am sending you to Timothy, my son whom I love..."
(I Corinthians 4:15-17)

As with Elisha and Elijah, Timothy was not Paul's natural son. Timothy's sonship was of spiritual birth. Timothy had become a son of Paul's through spiritual joining of the Lord. Sonship was not just something Timothy was to God, it was also a way that he was with Paul. If the Spirit of sonship is operational in our lives, we will become sons to whatever and whomever we touch. We will act as sons on the job, not as employees. We will act as sons in the congregation, not as hirelings. Sonship is something that begins from within and then flows out.

SONSHIP VS. SLAVERY

"For you did not receive a spirit that makes you a slave again to fear, but you received the Spirit of sonship. And by Him we cry, 'Abba Father.'" (Romans 8:15)

In this passage, the Apostle Paul contrasts the spirit of sonship with the spirit of slavery. These two spirits are two laws that operate within us. They frame the perspective from which we relate to God, ourselves, the church and everything we do. We either relate to life as a slave or as a son.

Man's natural tendency is to relate to God as a slave, not as a son. We see this exemplified in the life of the prodigal son. *"When he came to his senses, he said, 'How many of my father's hired men have food to spare, and here I am starving to death! I will set out and go back to my father and say to him: Father, I have sinned against heaven and against you. I am no longer worthy to be called your son, make me like one of your hired men."' (Luke 15:17-19)*

The inherent sense of guilt within the prodigal son caused him to relate to his father like a slave not as a son. The son did not say "I will return and be as a son." But rather, "I will return and be treated as a slave." The father did not view the prodigal as a slave; it was the son's problem, not the father's. Jesus Christ has made us worthy. Because of His shed blood we can enter Father's presence with boldness and act as sons, not slaves. We need not subject ourselves to feelings of inferiority or unworthiness because our relationship to Father is not about us, but Him. It is all a result of Christ's finished work.

The Transfer of Sonship

As parents we must bring our children out of the phase of childhood and lead them into the phase of sonship. We must instill within them a sense of who they are by leading them into a personal knowledge of Jesus through the Holy Spirit. We must train them to see their natural tendency to relate to life as a slave and introduce them to the spirit of sonship.

We must train them to live their lives in complete dependency on the person of Jesus Christ. Central to the truth of sonship is the understanding that apart from Jesus, we can do nothing. Consequently, we must train our children to live a life yielded to the work of the Holy Spirit.

A major aspect of the Holy Spirit's work in our lives during the phase of sonship is integration. The slavish nature within us all seeks to keep us in a place of defensive independence. We are all at times *transitionally* independent, but slaves are *defensively* independent. Slaves will defend their independent nature and resist any attempt to integrate their lives into the unity of the body of Christ.

In the margin notes of Romans 8:15, the spirit of sonship is also called the spirit of adoption. To be adopted is to have been on the outside and then integrated into a family. The spirit of adoption is contrary to the spirit of independence. The spirit of adoption seeks integration, not independence. As created beings we are created by God to yield. Yielding is part of our created design. The issue is not whether we will yield to something or remain independent. The issue is, will what we yield to, bring us into a deeper understanding of sonship, or will it foster the spirit of slavery?

"God sets the lonely in families..." (Psalm 68:6) The Hebrew word here for "families" means, "to be on the inside."[9] The heart-desire of Father is to take those who are on the outside and bring them into the security of belonging to a family. I used to argue against the idea that we had an inner circle and an outer circle. Now I understand that God recognizes the existence of both circles and seeks to bring all of His sons and daughters into the inner circle. That is, He seeks to bring all within the circle of family. I no longer try to defend the accusation that there is an outer circle. I acknowledge its legitimate existence and spend my energies making sure everyone feels welcomed to come into the security of the spiritual family.

As a parent I must seek to instill in my children the biblical necessity to reject isolation. They must seek to be integrated into their natural family as well as their spiritual family.

To be part of a family is to yield to the spirit of adoption, bringing us into the complete embrace of the whole, not the isolation of a part. I Corinthians 12:13 speaks of the baptism into the body of Christ. Father's desire is to baptize the lives of His sons and daughters into each other. That is, He seeks to immerse our lives into each other's lives. Here is where we discover if we believe in baptism by immersion or by sprinkling. As good charismatics, we will say we believe in baptism through immersion, that is, until we speak of the baptism of the body of Christ. Then, just a little sprinkle will do. Without the full integration of the other members of God's family, we stand the risk of never reaching our full potential, but remaining half the person we were designed to be.

THE CHROMOSOMAL EMBRACE

In her book, *Men and Microscopes*,[10] Katherine Shipper makes some commonly understood statements in the natural that have some profound spiritual applications. She says, "When the egg is fertilized by the sperm the slender threads of chromosomes twist around each other in what is calledthe chromosomal embrace."[19]

God's created design of the natural body has spiritual application as well.

Father desires His sons and daughters to embrace each other in unity with a sense of belonging, allowing the fullness of His created design to be fully realized. Katherine Shipper proceeds, saying, "It's the combination of the genes that determine the character of the new individual, an organism that is new, for it bears a new combination of genes, yet old for it is composed of the same material passed down from generation to generation."[12]

Without the embracing of integration we stand the risk of remaining half an identity. The spiritual application of the chromosomal embrace happens when I allow the Holy Spirit to join me to another, and God's deposit in the other's life is imparted to me. I then become a God-ordained combination of His life in them and His life in me.

Have you ever given yourself to chromosomal embrace? Have you led your children into the understanding of and the actual embrace?

Sonship is Phase II of generational transfer. Within this phase are the 2nd and 3rd stages of spiritual growth that must be imparted to those who follow. Remember this Stage One of our spiritual growth was responsibility in Phase I, childhood.

Stage Two: Apprenticeship

Responsibility was the stage where, "I'll do, you watch." Apprenticeship is the next stage where "We do together." A return to the ancient path is a return to the practice of bringing the generations alongside of each other for the purpose of emulation and imitation.

The picture of apprenticeship is a son growing up alongside of his father, learning what his grandfather knows, by imitating what his father does. Apprenticeship is the essence of discipleship.

"And the things you have heard me say in the presence of many witnesses entrust to reliable men who will also be qualified to teach others." (II Timothy 2:2)

Paul charged Timothy with the responsibility of apprenticing faithful sons who would also apprentice faithful sons, who in turn would also apprentice faithful sons… And so the mandate of generational transfer is fully realized.

The Joining of Wisdom and Zeal

Apprenticeship is the joining of wisdom and zeal. It joins the wisdom of the older generation with the zeal of the younger. Age brings with it tremendous wisdom. It is the wisdom of experience gleaned through years of real life. But experience often causes us to become a bit faded. The willingness to risk often wanes in the knowledge of experience. Consequently, the wisdom of experience is often constrained by the apathy of old age.

Youth brings with it tremendous zeal. Inherent in the enthusiasm of our youthful years is the desire to be daring and adventurous. The problem is that zeal is not always accompanied with wisdom. Consequently, youth who are led by zeal alone find themselves in consistent trouble. God's answer to this dilemma is the joining of the generations. In this generational joining we experience the marriage of wisdom and zeal. What often comes with age is enhanced by the zeal of youth and the foolishness of youth is tempered by the wisdom that comes with age. A return to the ancient path is a return to wisdom and zeal walking side by side, thus gaining the power and respect of generational joining.

DUAL RESPONSIBILITY

Apprenticeship requires a dual responsibility; it involves both giving and receiving. For apprenticeship to accomplish its God-desired result, fathers must have a vision to give and sons must have the vision to receive. Apprenticeship means a father's heart given to his son and a son's heart turned toward his father.

The Isaac generation is a generation of apprentices. The Isaac generation is the second-generation ministries that have been trained by the Abrahams in order that they might produce the Jacobs. The Isaac generation is a generation characterized by a deep level of trust in the sovereign Lord God. It is the generation willing to yield to the leading of their Abrahams, knowing that God will provide a lamb. The blessing of the Isaac generation is realized in the power of inheritance. The Isaac generation receives all Abraham had, as well as all that they will be enabled to do. Though I am a first generation Christian, I have second-generation ministry. I am an Abraham in the faith and an Isaac in the ministry. I had the privilege of being trained for ministry by a father in the faith who imparted to me over 40 years of ministry experience into my youthful zeal. Consequently, when we planted Christ Church Kirkland in 1985, we hit the ground running. Not only did we begin Day One with a substantial physical inheritance, more importantly, we started with a rich spiritual inheritance. So much had already been invested in us that though we were only one day old, we had a sense of being well established. Worship was intimate, discipline was evident, teaching was strong, and commitment was proven. We did have a need though. We needed tremendous growth, but we had a sure foundation because our Abraham had passed us an invaluable inheritance.

The pride of desiring to be original robs the church from the inheritance of the Isaac generation. The church has drunk deeply from the well of origination. Subsequently, we have strayed from the ancient path of replication. Every generation tends to establish its own way rather than inheriting the way of the fathers who have gone before. Jesus, the Pattern-Son, found His life and authority in replicating all He saw His Father doing. He never sought to establish His own way. Rather His goal was to emulate all He saw in His Father and work only where He saw His Father working.

The power of apprenticeship is found in the mandate of representation. Jesus was the exact representation of His Father. *(Hebrews 1:3)* Who or what are you representing? A return to the ancient path is a return to the mandate of representation. To represent something is to re-present it. To represent Jesus is to say again what He already said and be again who He is.

Jesus Christ is our primary representation. But, if the spirit of representation is in us, we will also seek to represent those we have been called to become apprentices to. Being faithful representatives of them proves and qualifies us to become spiritual fathers to others.

"And if you have not been trustworthy with someone else's property, who will give you property of your own?" (Luke 16:12)
It is in representing the vision of our spiritual fathers that we are qualified to steward our own vision.

My Personal Testimony
Twenty-five years ago I was the janitor of the church. I am now Senior Leader. In 1975 I was hired as the janitor of Faith Temple, Seattle Washington. I served in that janitorial capacity for a little over two years,

during which time and in the twelve subsequent years, I learned what it was to serve the vision Father had placed in another man. There were times that I did not fully understand the vision and at times did not agree with the vision, but I did understand the limitations of my perspective and the necessity to be faithful with what belonged to someone else.

Little did I know then how the sovereign plan of God would unfold as I was found trustworthy with someone else's property. I was progressively given responsibility of my own. Twenty-five years later I now serve as Senior Leader to those same pastors and many of the people I served as janitor.

The key to my preparation was the joy I found being apprenticed. I will forever be indebted to Jim Hamann who took me in as a son and allowed me to become an apprentice to him in the ministry. For over twenty-five years I have had the privilege of walking alongside of him, learning from the depth of his experience. Like an Isaac, I have received a rich inheritance from Pastor Jim.

For the past fourteen years, Pastor Jim and Phyllis have been in our congregation at Christ Church Kirkland. Even though I have served as the Senior Leader for the past twenty years, Jim still calls me every Sunday morning at 7:00am to pray for me and encourage me in the faith before I go to preach.

STAGE THREE: STEWARDSHIP

Phase I of generational transfer is childhood. In this phase of generational transfer we discover our first stage of spiritual growth, responsibility. Phase II of generational transfer is sonship, in which we discover our second and third stages of spiritual growth, apprenticeship and stewardship.

Stewardship is the stage where "You do, I'll watch." Stewardship is the stage in our spiritual development where we come of age and own truth for ourselves. It's the stage where we are given "property" of our own, (*Luke 16:12*) and are expected to multiply what we have been given.

It is in the stage of stewardship that sonship and the reality of generational transfer is proven, for it is here that the opportunity to abandon the way is greatest. Will we seek to establish a new way? Or will we remain faithful to the ancient path as passed down from our forefathers?

HUMANISTIC DECEPTION

As sons and daughters of the Kingdom we must discern the humanistic deception in how truth is transferred. Humanism says, "You are of age, now you must discover your own truth and establish your own way. In contrast, the ancient path of the Kingdom of God says, "Truth is passed generationally, so now that you are of age you must continue in the way of the ancient path." In the Kingdom of God the truth of the fathers is also the truth of the sons, for there is only one truth. The way of the fathers is also the way of the sons, for there is only one way.

Inherent in humanistic reasoning is the suggestion that our father's truth began with them so we have the right to establish our own love of truth and pursue our own way. But the truth of the Kingdom of God is not found in establishing our own truth. Rather, it is being a steward of our father's truth and becoming responsible to the generations past in order that we might equip the generations to come.

THREE PRINCIPLES OF STEWARDSHIP

1. We own nothing, for everything belongs to the Lord. Our life ended at Calvary. Our old lives were buried with the Lord in the waters of baptism. Consequently, everything we are and all that we have is a stewardship. The Lord entrusted us with it all as stewards, not as owners.

Such is the case with the generations. Our children belong to the Lord. They are given to us as a trust. Our responsibility is to raise them according to the mandate of trust. The principles of God's Word in relationship to child training are the principles we are to follow. Culture will offer us an alternative. Circumstances may even challenge our way. But since parenting is a stewardship, we must remain faithful to the mandate given.

2. Our lives are given to us with an expectation of increase.

The parable of the ten talents reveals God's heart for increase. A trust is not given to us to hoard but is given with the expectation that over time, we will increase whatever was given. The increase is measured both in terms of quantity and quality. Though we are not always given control over the quantity of increase, we can determine its quality. In the case of children, God controls the womb. We do not determine the quantity of our family's increase, but we can address the quality of that increase.

Time spent with our children, worldview, biblical training... are all factors that determine the quality of their increase.

3. Our increase is to be freely distributed as the Holy Spirit directs.

We serve in a backward Kingdom. To keep something in the Kingdom of God, we must give it away. We must raise the generations with a desire to be spent in service to the King. They must find their lives in service to their God-given destiny. Only in serving the eternal purpose for their lives will they find the joy of fulfillment. In losing their lives to the Kingdom of God, they will find their lives.

Being an example in our parenting is the key to this principle of stewardship. Our children must see in our example the demonstration of a life lost in service to the eternal purpose.

Parents must lead their families by the principle of mandate, not self-desire. Because we are stewarding what belongs to Jesus, we must steward it the way He wants it stewarded. We must steward generationally. Humanism says everybody must discern truth on their own; they must find their own way and discover their own vision. Humanism says truth is not generational, for yesterday's truth belongs to yesterday and today's truth belongs to today.

A return to the ancient path is embracing the understanding that truth is generational, for it is rooted in God's eternal purpose. (*Ephesians 2:11*) Though there may be many ways in terms of method, there is only one way in terms of truth. (*John 14:6*) There really is only one way, and this way will remain consistent throughout the generations. One generation may change the method of the former, but the content remains eternal.

Stewardship embraces the validity of the ancient way and passes that way on to the next generation.

PHASE III—FATHERHOOD

Fatherhood is the phase in our spiritual journey that best captures the mandate of generational transfer. Fatherhood is all about reproduction. Without reproduction there is no generational transfer, for without reproduction there would be no generation in which to transfer. Fatherhood is a phase that all are intended to achieve but not many do. The preoccupation with self that permeates our day has circumvented the cycle of reproduction. Self prevents the sacrifice necessary to reproduce.

Fatherhood is the stage in our journey where we do for another. In childhood we embraced the stage of "I'll do, you watch." Sonship brought us to, "We do together," and "You do, I'll watch." Now fatherhood brings us to that place of maturity where, "We do for another."

Fatherhood in the Kingdom of God is a description, not a position. Fatherhood is the result of a labor done. It is not a title assigned to a person. I am a father in the Kingdom only to the degree that my spiritual genes have been reproduced in those God has brought into my life. If the reasoning, gifting and burdens that the sovereignty of God has birthed in me are not birthed in them as well, I am not their spiritual father. I may be someone they respect or deeply admire, but I am not their father. I may be their guardian or even their teacher, but not their father. If the spiritual genes Father has placed in me are duplicated in them, only then am I their father.

Guardians Teach; Fathers Impart

"I am not writing this to shame you, but to warn you, as my dear children. Even though you have ten thousand guardians in Christ, you do not have many fathers, for in Christ Jesus I became your father through the gospel. Therefore I urge you to imitate me. For this reason I am sending to you Timothy, my son whom I love, who is faithful in the Lord. He will remind you of my way of life in Christ Jesus, which agrees with what I teach everywhere in every church." (I Corinthians 4:14-17)

"I became your father." Paul's fatherhood in Corinth was not positional or automatic. Paul became their father. He became their father as a result of his his spiritual genes being reproduced in them. Fatherhood in the Kingdom is a descriptive title, not a positional one. The reason Paul said, *"You may have ten thousand guardians, but not many fathers,"* was simply because there are not many who are willing to bear the responsibility of reproduction. Built into the function of reproduction is the responsibility of risk. Reproduction

requires a time for intimacy. It means the possibility of being hurt. These factors and others diminish the number of those willing to bear the responsibility to reproduce. Teaching is perceived to be the easier way. Guardians teach, but fathers impart life. Anyone or anything else can teach. Computers teach, television can teach, but it takes a father to reproduce life. Fathers do not just instruct, they impart. Fathers are willing to get close to their sons and daughters and are willing to open their lives to those in their care.

"I urge you to imitate me." (I Corinthians 4:16) That is a statement of reproduction. A statement of a father speaking to his spiritual sons and daughters. Paul is not speaking of the imitation of mannerisms, but the imitation of God's deposit in his life. Imitating the will and way of God in a spiritual father brings life. Imitation is automatic, if we permit it. Once the spiritual genes are sown, they will automatically reproduce themselves if we do not let the pride of originality circumvent the natural design.

"I am sending Timothy my Son... he will remind you of my way." (I Corinthians 4:17) Implied in this verse is the fact that Paul had a defined way. Peter had his ways and John had his ways. But the Corinthians were sons of Paul. So Paul was reminding them that they were the reproductive result of his genes.

You have become a father when your spiritual genes have been reproduced in another. You need not define these genes and write the performance code to prove the reproduction. If reproduction has happened, it will reveal itself in your sons.

But what about Matthew 23:9 that says, "Don't call anyone on earth 'father'" Fatherhood is a phase not necessarily needing a title, rather, it is the recognition of function and responsibility. To label someone with the title of father is not the issue. The issue is for fathers to fulfill the mandate of reproduction and for sons to receive a father's heart as it is given. Obviously, Jesus was addressing something far deeper in His admonition of Matthew 23:9. Jesus was after the prideful attitude of the Pharisees who prided themselves in their positions and flaunted their titles, but they were void of any function. If the directive not to call anyone "Father," was a literal directive, then Paul would have been in sin when he said that he became the father to the Corinthians.

CHRIST-LIKENESS IS REALIZED IN FATHERHOOD

The goal of our Christian walk is to become Christlike. To be like Christ is to be a father. Jesus the Child-born, became the Son given, but He is now the everlasting Father. To be like Christ is to press deeply enough into our gifting and calling that we become reproducers of that which God has given us.

In his book, *The Masculine Journey,*[13] Robert Hicks defined six Hebrew words that in English are interpreted as man, describing them as chronological stages we pass through in our "masculine journey."

> Adam: Man in the generic sense, male and female, man as the created being.

> Zakar: Man in his base, anatomical state. It is this word that gives man his sexual distinction from woman.

> Gobbor: Man as a warrior, man in his warring strength and competitive nature.

> Enosh: Man as the wounded warrior, describes man in his weakness and frailty.

> Ish: Man as ruler, man contrasted with youth, adult man, man who has overcome Enosh.

> Zaken: Man as elder at the gate, mentor, sage, man as the father of Israel who imparts wisdom at the city gate to the young who sit at his feet.

The goal of every child born, and the challenge of every son given, is to become "Zaken." The goal is to become a reproducer of the entrustments God has placed within each of us. The laws of Kingdom stewardship require increase and reproduction. Only in reproduction is generational transfer realized.

Generational transfer is the mandate of every believer. Whether it be to the natural born sons and daughters or to those sons and duaghters born through the Spirit, we must pass to those who are placed in our care, the spiritual genes given to us. Without this transfer, we are left with a generation without identity. A generation without identity is a generation without purpose and direction. We must return to the ancient path and thus return to spiritual reproduction.

FOOTNOTES:

9. Strong's Concordance
10. Shipper, Katherine, Men & Microscopes, pg. 181
11. Shipper, Katherine, Men & Microscopes, pg. 181
12. Shipper, Katherine, Men & Microscopes, pg. 181
13. Roberts Hicks, The Masculine Journey. (It is my understanding that Robert Hicks Masculine Journey has come under considerable scrutiny as to its Biblical accuracy. It is not my intent to support the position or deny it. The intent is simply to underscore the importance of every believer growing from child to reproducer. Whether Hicks position is an accurate support for this is open for discussion, but what is clear is the need to reproduce the life of Christ in us, in order for the process of generational transfer to occur.)

FAMILIES *of* DESTINY

THOUGH DESTINY IS THE BIRTHRIGHT of every believer, it is not a guarantee. Though it is a predetermined course established by the sovereignty of God, it is not a guaranteed contract. To fulfill the destiny determined for us as individuals and as a family, we must apprehend it and purposefully engage it. Divine initiative must meet up with human responsibility. *"Before I formed you in the womb I knew you, before you were born I set you apart. I appointed you to be a prophet to the nations." (Jeremiah 1:5)*

A CALL TO DESTINY

Jeremiah's call was a call to destiny. Long before Jeremiah was born, Father had already determined what His destiny would be. The initiation had nothing to do with Jeremiah; the execution most certainly required his cooperation.

Webster defines destiny as, "an appointed or predetermined condition established by divine decree." To become a family of destiny means we are families who are seeking after and living according to the predetermined conditions established by God.

"For we are God's workmanship, created in Christ Jesus to do good works, which God prepared in advance for us to do." (Ephesians 2:10)

To seek destiny is simply to seek after the work God has already prepared in advance for us to do. Ultimate effectiveness and anointing is found in this work, for it is in His work that we can say as Jesus did, *"I only work where I see my Father working." (John 5:19)*

Destiny is not something reserved just for the individual. As an individual with destiny is placed into a family, that family becomes a family of destiny. The church universal is the family of God. Even as the church universal family has an appointed and predetermined condition so does each individual family. It is the destiny of the family universal that determines the scope of the destiny of the family specific. So it is not a matter of determining our own destiny for our family, rather it is discerning our families' predetermined plan.

THE STARTING POINT

The starting point of a family of destiny is not the family itself. The starting point for a family of destiny is the Kingdom of God. To live in pursuit of destiny is to live, not pursuing ourselves, but something bigger than ourselves. To make the family the starting point is to start too small. Our starting point must be some place outside ourselves, lest we limit the scope of our destiny and make it self-related.

In the Kingdom of God the flow of life is outward, not inward. We find real life as we reach out from ourselves, not ministering only to ourselves. A family that makes its central focus inward on the family itself is a family that has missed the essence of the Kingdom of God. In the Kingdom of God a family must lose itself in order to find itself.[14] Real life for the family is found as the family learns to live for something bigger than itself.

Because life flows outward, individuals find their lives in the family, the family finds its life in the church and the church finds its life in the Kingdom. I have not only seen destinies destroyed because families were given no apparent honor or focus, but I have seen destinies destroyed because the family was given too much honor and focus. If our enemy cannot keep us from a Kingdom truth, he will try to drive us past the truth. The Word of God never instructs us to seek the family or to put it first. Jesus said, *"Seek first the Kingdom and its righteousness and everything else will be added to you." (Matthew 6:33)* In this, "everything" includes becoming a family of destiny. The starting point to becoming a family of destiny is the absolute surrender to the government of the Kingdom of God. As we yield to Christ's government by way of submission and surrender, our cry for family will be fulfilled by Him.

TWO PERSPECTIVES ON DESTINY

Though destiny is a predetermined condition, it is not a guaranteed contract. We do not earn our destiny, but we do work for it. The work is not a striving by our own natural strength, but it is a labor of exchange. Paul frames it quite clearly in Colossians 1:29 *"To this end I labor, struggling with all His energy which so powerfully works in me."* Yes it is a labor, but it is a labor of exchanged strength.

Destinies are not automatic. They are predetermined conditions that are received over time through obedient actions and godly behavior. Our destiny is His plan, accomplished in His strength, but realized by our work.

Consequently, destinies can be either built or destroyed. Self-will yielded to the will of God will build a destiny. Self-will lived contrary to the will of God will destroy destiny.

Destiny Builders

I. Covenantal Obedience

"...If you follow my decrees, carry out my regulations and keep all my commands and obey them, I will fulfill through you the promise I gave to David your father." (I Kings 6:12)

Destinies are built through daily obedience to the covenantal way of the Lord. While the love of God is unconditional, destiny is quite conditional. Our destinies are fulfilled upon the condition of daily obedience to the decrees and regulations spoken to us by the Lord. Involved conditions are both the written decrees in the Scriptures and the spoken decrees the Holy Spirit has given us as personal and family distinctives.

To the degree Solomon kept these decrees, he prospered and his throne flourished. But when these decrees were broken through the marrying of foreign wives and the adopting of their practices, his throne was undermined.

History reveals that one of the greatest challenges throughout time has been the generational transfer of the covenantal way. The Holy Spirit reveals a particular truth to a prior generation, but the generation following often struggles to continue in that way. It is through the embracing of that particular way that the prior generation prospers, so when the next generation does not continue in that way, prosperity is lost and destiny is destroyed. Usually this takes place through neglect by the prior generation to whom the Holy Spirit reveals a certain truth. The generation to come is always full of idealistic zeal and sacrificial passion. If this zeal and passion is captured early enough, the next generation will have no problem in their willingness to embrace the way and live up to the standard. But often the parents, feeling like the children won't be willing to live up to the same revelation they have received, reduce their expectations and, in doing so, fail to capture their zeal and passion and thus lose the next generation.

The American Puritans illustrated this dilemma. Fearing their children would not embrace the standard of expectation required of the Lord for them, they developed what became known as the "halfway covenant." This was simply a reduced portion of all that the Lord required of them. The problem was, it was a man-made covenant. *"Except the Lord build the house, they labor in vain who build it." (Psalm 127:1)* In reducing the covenant, they were unable to capture the zeal and passion of their youth, so they went their own way.

The generations to come are created by God to be idealistic and passionate. If these ideals and passions are not directed towards the purposes of God, the future generations will be redirected by the ways of this world. It is certain, if we do not captivate their ideals, something else will. As parents, we must never be ashamed of the high standard of biblical expectation. Conversely, we must never add to biblical expectation and lose the generation through religion and legalism.

Biblical expectations and the covenantal way are supplied full of grace to help us walk in that way. It is not a heavy yoke for the coming generation to bear. When the generation to come is introduced to the joy of personal relationship to Jesus Christ and a commitment to the cause He brings, their ideals and their zeal are fully employed. Leading our children into experience will carry them only for a season. But leading and bringing them into eternal destiny will require embracing the person of Jesus Christ in His fullness and the willingness to embrace the full covenant with all its expectations and all of its grace. Compromise will never suffice.

2. Early Rising

"How can a young man keep his way pure? By living according to your word. I seek you with all my heart; do not let me stray from your commands. I have hidden your word in my heart that I might not sin against you." (Psalm 119:9-11)

Destiny begins with an intimate, personal relationship with Jesus Christ. Without that intimate relationship, life is empty and void of true fulfillment. Our children must be led into a personal discovery of Jesus and His sovereign rule over their lives. "That I might know Him" needs to be their heart's cry.[15]

Destiny is a predetermined condition—a predetermined condition that the

Bible says is higher than our ways and is, in fact, quite the opposite of our own ways. The Kingdom of God is a backward Kingdom. In the Kingdom of God the way up is down. To keep something we must give it away. To find our lives, we must first lose them.

To learn of this predetermined destiny requires much time in the presence of the Lord. It is only as we behold Him that our lives are transformed into His likeness and we learn His ways.[16]

Children learn best by example. (More is caught than taught.) As parents, both physical and spiritual, we must train our children by our example, teaching them the value of rising early and seeking the way of the Lord. Such training will require time—our time. Children do not desire this naturally. Most parents are not willing to invest the time required to give this training to their children, thinking it requires too much. But these same parents are willing to spend hours training their children in soccer, ballet and other sports-related areas without the least concern about time. If we place a high value on something, time is of little concern. But for the sake of destiny, we must redefine our value and be willing to invest the time necessary to train ourselves, and our children, in the privilege of rising early to seek the Lord. We will discuss some practicals on this issue in Chapter 10.

3. Biblical Worldview

"I pray also that the eyes of your heart may be enlightened in order that you may know the hope to which He has called you..." (Ephesians 1:18)

Destiny building begins with the perspective that we have been apprehended for Him. Our lives are not our own; we exist for Him. Consequently, we are first Christ's inheritance, so our perspectives and pursuits must focus on, and center, in Him.

In accepting Christ, not only do we receive a Savior, we also receive a Kingdom. Jesus Christ is a King with a Kingdom. His government is both a government and a particular way. A biblical worldview is a view of life that starts with Christ and His Kingdom. It is the choice to view all of life and its circumstances through the eyes of Jesus as revealed in His Word. Decisions, circumstances and beliefs are all interpreted through the Word of God.

Children must be trained to interpret life through a biblical grid. We must train them to think biblically, rather than culturally. We must train them to yield to the way of the Lord when that way cuts across culture or across their personal desire. To do so, we as parents must know the Scriptures and how they are to be applied to life's situations. We must study to show ourselves approved.[17]

4. Living a life of sacrifice

"Whoever finds his life will lose it and whoever loses his life for my sake will find it." (Matthew 10:39)

The road to destiny is paved with the stones of personal sacrifice. This does not mean that destiny requires self-induced poverty or legalistic externals. Living a life of sacrifice is living a life yielded to Christ as the owner of our life. That ownership translates into needing more of Him and less of us. When a life is yielded as a sacrifice to Him, all that remains is Christ in us.

Parents must train the generations to come to see personal sacrifice as a virtue rather than something to be avoided. It is an extreme honor to sacrifice our time, resources and gifts for the purposes of God. We parents must train our children to give their lives away through service and Kingdom availability, for only in the giving of our lives away will we find our lives.

Christ Church Kirkland was founded in 1985. To come on full time to lead the church, we took well over a fifty-percent per year cut in pay. It was an extreme financial sacrifice, but Marcy and I considered it an honor to make that sacrifice for the purposes of the Lord. As that decision was made and other opportunities of sacrifice have come up, we have trained our children to see them as a privilege, not a burden. We have also been careful to tie every blessing we receive in ministry back to the favor of the Lord in order for them to see that ministry involves both sacrifice and reward.

Living a life of sacrifice produces those who know how to embrace responsibility. Often the criticism of the coming generation is their irresponsibility. Irresponsibility is a destiny thief! Living a life of sacrifice teaches our children that they are not the center of existence. Irresponsibility is most often the result of selfish thinking. Irresponsible decisions are made because the decision-makers based their decisions purely on themselves.

When children have been raised under the lifestyle of sacrificial living, they tend to think of others before themselves. Their decisions are made from the basis of how they will impact the purposes of God, not themselves. The results are responsible decisions and the ability to carry responsibility, producing leadership for the next generation.

Many times I have had people ask me, "What was the key to your leadership development?" Outside of my personal relationship and devotion to Christ, my answer has been simply this: "Embrace responsibility." By embracing responsibility, we move deeper into our destiny and become more productive in our service to the Lord. I wish I could say I have done what I have done purely because of my love for Jesus Christ, but I cannot. Often when my emotions said no, my will has said yes—simply because the responsibility I was carrying required it. Certainly our goal is to respond out of love and devotion to Christ, but until that happens, responsibility will carry us.

5. Christ-centeredness

The destiny of God is found in the person of Jesus Christ. Our destiny is realized and built to the degree we place Him at the center of our lives. For it is *"in Him we live and move and have our being..." (Acts 17:28)* When our lives are lived with Him as the center of our pursuit, our destiny is realized. When our lives are lived with ourselves as the center, our destiny is robbed. We are His inheritance. We exist to serve His purpose and fulfill His calling.

This truth is the most basic and most fundamental truth as pertaining to our destiny in Jesus. If we live accordingly, we will be used and our joy will be complete.

UNDERSTANDING THE TACTICS

It is vital to understand that many destiny destroyers cannot be argued against on the basis of sin or no sin. Destiny destroyers are far more subtle than that. When it comes to the fulfilling of our destiny, the issue is often not one of sin, but rather one of expedience. It may not be sinful to get involved in a particular matter, but will it serve to further our destiny or will it hinder it? Maturity demands that we make decisions on the basis of expedience, not what seems to be right and wrong. All things may be permissible, but all things are not expedient *(I Corinthians 6:12)*.

The Apostle Paul supports this in I Corinthians 13:11, as he said, *"When I became a man I put childish ways aside."* Childish ways are not necessarily sinful ways. It is certain that some are, but others are just immature. They serve as distractions that prevent our maturity and keep us as perpetual infants and unproductive to the purposes of God. These childish ways must be put aside in order for us to reach the fullness of God's desire and take hold of that for which we were apprehended.

The Apostle Paul addresses this issue of destiny destroyers again with the church in Galatia. *"You were running a good race. Who cut in on you and kept you from obeying the truth?" (Galations 5:7)* Most destiny destroyers begin as seemingly innocent distractions. They begin as, *"A little yeast ..." (Galatians 5:9)* But soon those little distractions become major strongholds that leaven the entire batch of dough.

Some begin as reactions to a perceived religious attitude, perhaps in reaction to legalism. In reaction to the stifling bondage of legalism, some cause us to form philosophies of reaction that simply exchange legalism for liberality. Generational transfer is a principal that works both for the good and for the bad. One generation's liberty becomes the next generation's license if that liberty is not substantiated on firm biblical ground. If liberality is substantiated simply by reaction to legalism rather than Scriptural permission, it will most definitely lead to license in the generation to come and work as the leaven to destroy its destiny.

Other destiny destroyers begin as attitudes of redefinition. Whether it is because some are ashamed of the Gospel or if they perceive that the expectations are too high, either way, they redefine what the Scriptures require and lessen their expectations. Central to other attitudes is the Word of God. Those who seek to redefine truth say, "The Bible contains the inerrant Word of God, but is not inerrant in its entirety." Once the inerrancy of the Scriptures is lost, everything is open for redefinition. Once the absolute standard is lost, everything becomes relative and open for personal opinion and application. Biblical expectations become "cultural expectations for the New Testament period only." The Ten Commandments become the "Ten

Suggestions." Everything moral is redefined through cultural lenses, until we are back to everyone doing that which is right in their own eyes.

Destiny Destroyers

I. Children left to themselves.

Parents today have been inundated with a fear of leadership. Parents are afraid to lead their children, afraid to say no, afraid to draw lines of expectation. The enemy has crafted a clever scheme that accuses any parent who leads as being controlling and abusive. Certainly there are those who are controlling and abusive, but to lead our children according to biblical expectations is far from being controlling or abusive.

The result of this fear to lead is that children are left to themselves. Many in their formative years do not learn the value of the word "no." So inevitably, they know little of the fear of God. Children left to themselves, grow up without lines of definition and protection and therefore, grow up insecure.

A child left to himself is not the way shown to us in the Scriptures. *"...A child left to himself disgraces his mother." (Proverbs 29:15)* Embarrassment and disgrace are both the result of a child left without boundary lines of leadership. Many times I have been in either a restaurant or grocery store only to see that public place taken hostage by a two or three-year-old left to itself. As the child screamed and hollered to get its way, it was as if the parent was completely oblivious to what was taking place. Every eye in the place was on the child, except the eye of the parent.

Recently I was in a toy store with my two sons. As we were looking at the toys, a small boy about three years old came in with his mother and father. Immediately, he started asking them for everything in the store. As his parents said *no*, he began to yell and scream in disappointment. The louder the child got, the more the parents ignored his screams. The more the parents ignored his screams for attention, the more exasperated the child became. Unable to get a reaction, the boy finally ran behind his mother and slugged her in the middle of her back. Both parents were completely aware of what took place, especially the mother, but neither parent said a word about the blatant disrespect. The mother did not reprimand her son for hitting, nor did the father take his place to protect his wife and assure her honor. The child left to himself certainly brought disrespect to his mother.

The wisdom of this world would tell us, "Well, children will be children." Yes, that may very well be true, but it is for that very reason that parents must be parents. If we are going to accept the fact that children will be children, then we must also embrace the truth of parents needing to be parents.

"I have chosen Abraham because he will command his children and his household after him to keep the way of the Lord..." (Genesis 18:19 KJV)

Abraham was chosen because of his willingness to lead. His way was not the way of suggestion, but the way of command. He commanded his children to keep the way of the Lord and it was that courage to lead that gained him the favor of the Lord. Abraham could take such a bold stand because he was not commanding his children to follow his self-determined way. He was commanding them to follow the way of the Lord. When we know the clearly defined way of the Lord, we can stand in our place of command and lead our children into their destinies.

Humanism tells us, "We cannot force our way upon our children; they must find their own way." This philosophy may have merit if the issue was our way verses their way, but the issue is neither our way nor their way. The issue is the way of the Lord. The Scriptures show us that God ordained the way for our children to follow. Not only is it acceptable for parents to command their children in the way of the Lord, we are mandated to do it. Our children do not belong to us but are an entrustment from the Lord. As an entrustment, we must be stewards according to the prescribed intention of the Rightful Owner. To do so will require the willingness to lead our children and not be afraid to cross their will when it is contrary to the will of the Lord.

Parents must recognize their responsibility before God to protect their children's destiny. They must be watchmen being careful of what comes in and what goes out of their children's eyes. Parents must be willing to protect their children from certain television programs and movies. Temptation and compromise are accessible as never before even being brought into our own homes. Watch out for sports programs as they are full of compromising commercials.

Parents must also protect their children from certain books. They must discern the friends they play with, for bad company does corrupt good morals.[18] Yes, for the the sake of evangelism our children must become friends with sinners but, as parents, we must discern who is influencing whom. When a relationship is having a negative influence on our children, we must provide the leadership necessary to make the appropriate change. Parents must be willing to protect their daughters from dressing immodestly. The fashion trends of the day must never be the determining factor of our children's dress. As dresses get shorter and necklines get lower, parents must be willing to say *no*. This is not to say that our children cannot dress fashionably, but for the sake of relevance and testimony, Christians should be fashionably alert. Now, when the current fashions help cause the defrauding of men, we must draw the line and say *no*. The temporary restraint will lead to their long-term freedom.

A child left to themselves will not naturally go the way of the Lord. Parents must lead their children in the way they are to follow, the way of devotion to God. They must lead their children into a prayer life and the study of God's Word. They must lead them into the making of proper choices. They must show them the way of love. *"Love never fails…" (I Corinthians 13:8)* Parents must teach and train their children to follow in that way.

2. Public Education

From the onset, allow me to say there is no Scripture or verse that directly forbids the sending of our children to public schools. Public education is not a sin. What is sinful is the abdicating of the parental responsibility of education to a godless system that no longer recognizes the supremacy of God and His ownership of our lives. In no case does the Bible place the primary responsibility of education on anyone but the parent. Yes, the parent may delegate that responsibility to someone more learned, but only in a relationship of shared responsibility. Deuteronomy 6 and Psalm 78 are biblical examples of educational responsibility falling on the jurisdiction of the family.

Humanism has given us public education as we know it today. It is certain that humanism is a religion and public schools are its sanctuary of worship. Those who embrace the public system send their children of destiny into a godless, amoral system that is neutral to the Kingdom of God at best and in most cases, hostile. Most would say, "Our school is not at all hostile." It may not appear to be hostile to Jesus and His way, but try putting a manger display up at Christmas! Try saying a prayer in the classroom. Try starting an after-school Bible club. In most schools, the Hindus can meet without interference as can the Muslims and Buddhists. But when the Christians try to meet, they are stopped with the argument of the "separation of church and state." While we support the separation of the State into church affairs, we do *not* support separating God from any state run function. The earth is the Lord's and His presence must be allowed to permeate all that we do.

The battle with the public education system is not against specific teachers or administration. There are godly teachers and staff who are called of God and strategically placed in specific schools. The battle is against the system of public education. It is against the principalities and powers that drive the system and systematically remove all mention of Jesus and the Kingdom of God. The public educational system is actually not neutral. The social architects behind it have an agenda. The ultimate issue driving their agenda is, "Who owns the children?" Biblically, we know the answer to this question is God, but the State believes it also has ownership rights to the children.

This fact is proven in the face of home schooling. In some places, home schooling is outlawed and parents do not have the right to fulfill their biblical mandate to educate their children. Where home schooling is permitted, most States require parents to register a "declaration of intent," notifying the school district of their decision. In either case, the underlying motivation behind these laws is the State's philosophy of ownership. Yes, I understand that in some cases these laws were written because some families were negligent in their parental duties, but these isolated cases of educational negligence do not warrant universal law.

Such is the case behind physical abuse. The occurrences of physical abuse at the hand of negligent parents are appalling. But the appalling abuse is not justification for the right of the Child Protective Services (CPS) to come into one's home and remove the children at the State's discretion. A family can even be wrongfully accused and the CPS will remove the children until the accusations are substantiated. Parents are considered guilty until proven innocent. Why? Because the State believes it owns our children.

In light of the State's humanistic agenda, believing they own our children, your public school cannot be a neutral institution. You send your children into that godless system eight hours a day to be trained by a philosophy that is in most cases diametrically opposed to the Kingdom of God. At home you teach them to deny self, at school they are taught to love self. At home you teach them to prefer others, at school they are taught to take care of number one. At home you teach that the Kingdom of God is the central issue of life and should be openly shared with all. At school they are taught that religion is something deeply personal and should be kept to oneself.

The comparisons could go on and on. Though some are inconsequential, others are a matter of spiritual life and death. Yes, many have gone through the public system and have not lost their salvation. But it could also be argued that many have gone through the public system and have lost their destiny. In their most formative years, they were fed a godless, self-centered agenda and it left them dead to the purposes of God and void of a spiritual destiny. A Time magazine article stated that the average father spends seventeen seconds a day of uninterrupted time with his children. Compare those seventeen seconds with the hours spent daily in the public educational system and you tell me whose agenda is being communicated?

I realize that some argue their case for public schools on the basis of evangelism. While this is a noble and even worthy argument, I wonder "At what cost?" What has it cost our children in regard to their destiny to send them into an unbiblical system in the hopes of evangelism? This argument could perhaps work if the children were being specifically trained to reject humanism and how to influence their classmates with the truth of the Gospel of Jesus Christ. Unfortunately, most are not being trained like that, so they become the influenced, rather than the influencer, and in doing so their destinies are hindered. Many have argued that if all Christians pulled out of the public school system, there would be no opportunities for the children to witness or no light left in the system to influence. Being that I have home schooled our children, we have found that there are still plenty of opportunities for our children to witness. Whether it is with neighborhood friends, sport teams, work associates or unplanned encounters, they have plenty of opportunities to witness.

To address the issue of someone being light remaining in the system as an influence, my response is twofold. First, does the system need to be influenced or be allowed to die a natural death? Second, there are plenty of Christian teachers in public schools who hold positions of influence and have already settled issues of temptation of being better lights of influence than risking our children's destiny to do so.

Ultimately, the final argument of our involvement simply comes down to this. By placing our children in the public system, are we fulfilling our biblical mandate of responsibility, or are we abdicating our educational responsibility to someone else? Our stewardship accountability for our children will not be based on how they excelled in sports or whether they attended the right schools. Our accountability before God will be on whether or not we led them into the fullness of their destiny and sufficiently equipped them for their Kingdom purpose. The training and equipping of the coming generation rests in the hands of the fathers.

"Fathers do not exasperate your children, instead, bring them up in the training and instruction of the Lord." (Ephesians 6:4)

3. Dating

The challenge for the church throughout the ages has been the ability to think and act in a Kingdom way rather than the culture's way. Living in our culture twenty-four hours a day makes it quite easy to adopt the cultural practices and dress them up with Christian overtones. The battle of cultural practices versus Kingdom practice is quite subtle, but nevertheless deadly. The Apostle Paul warns us of this battle when he says in Romans 12:2, *"Do not conform any longer to the pattern of this world, but be transformed by the renewing of your mind."* Notice the tense in which the apostle speaks. The Christians in Rome had already conformed to a certain degree, but now he was pleading with them to do it no longer. The squeeze of conformity is so subtle that we are often drawn into the conformity before we even realize that we have strayed from biblical norms, having adopted cultural practices in their place.

Such is the case with our cultural concept of dating. Dating, as most have come to know it, is purely a cultural practice with absolutely no Scriptural precedent to substantiate it.

The practice of giving our heart, emotion and devotion on a trial basis, not just to one, but to many, has no Scriptural ground of support. It is purely a cultural practice that has left many with broken hearts, shattered emotions, loss of virginity and a fear to ever make a commitment again.

Yes, your experience with dating may have been nothing but a positive experience for you, but inspite of its positive nature for you, you still cannot support it biblically. At no level does the Bible support our current concept of dating. The dating concept, as most know it, is nothing more than practicing divorce. One gives his or her heart and emotions to the other, until something comes along to cross the will, and soon the relationship is over, only for the cycle to start again. By the time we get to the person of God's choice for us, we have been through multiple relationships and now carry the scars and baggage of each. It is into our marriages that we bring this baggage, that sooner or later must be sorted out lest it stays within us to fester and destroy our relationship.

Dating is not the biblical model. The biblical model is courtship, where one's heart is given to another only in pursuit of marriage and covenant. Everything about God and His way is covenantal. He does not make covenant and then "break up" with those He has made covenant with. Our culture has diverted us from our covenantal base and left us practicing its ways and eating its fruit.

As parents who are required by God to steward His children, we must realize that the dating model automatically awakens desires in our children that we cannot permit them to fulfil. We expect our teenage children to be mature enough to get their emotional motors running, but not put their physical desires in gear. Have we forgotten what our physical desires were when we were that age? You might argue that they can be trained to overcome. I am not suggesting that they cannot be trained to overcome. What I am suggesting is, why should they be trained to overcome? Dating is a model that sets our children up to fail. It leaves many with broken hearts and a divided eye. At the age when most begin dating, their eye should be wholly on the Lord, not on the opposite sex. If our goal is apprehending the destiny predetermined by the Lord, dating is nothing but a diversion designed to distract them from their purpose and calling.

How will our children get to know their future mate? Whenever I speak on the issue of courtship, this question is the first asked. The question reveals how culturized we have become. This world's pattern has so squeezed us into its mold that we think the only way we can meet and get to know someone is through dating. The problem is when dating is the means to a deeper relationship, emotions lead the way. So the emotions of each are known, but the dating model does not provide for the real person, the spiritual person to be known by each other. In the courtship model, the two people know each other as friends long before they open their emotions to each other. They meet at youth group or at school or on the job and they develop a friendship. They spend time with each other in the group setting, observing first their devotion to Jesus Christ. They seek to determine if Jesus is the primary pursuit of the other person's life, knowing that if the person they are thinking of is not seeking first the Kingdom of God and its righteousness, he or she would not make a suitable life partner.

Through courtship, they also seek to determine how the other person interacts with their family and friends. Also, are the fruits of the Spirit evident in their life? Are the gifts of the Spirit operational? Does the other carry a sense of Divine calling? Is he or she a spiritual son or daughter? Do they know who they are, why they are here and where they are going? Are there issues of generational sin evident in their behavior?

All of these questions and many others must be determined before the door of emotions is even opened. All of these are easily discerned in a group setting. If these questions are satisfied, the person must ask, "Are we old enough to enter into a relationship designed to end in marriage?" In the courtship model, hearts are given to each other only when in pursuit of marriage and covenant making. If one or the other parties is neither old enough or mature enough to handle the responsibilities of covenant making, then to enter into courship is premature.

If both parties are old enough and mature enough, they should consult with their parents before consulting with each other. The man should go to his father (presuming his father is alive) and consult with his father for advice and approval. He should then go to his Pastor and get any insight and approval his Pastor might have. If both the parents and the Pastor give their blessing, he should then contact the parents of the woman and seek their blessing.

At this point, if her parents give him their blessing, he then goes to the woman and asks her if she would consider entering into a courting relationship with him. By now she has known this man as a friend, because they have spent time with each other in group settings and have talked and conversed along the way. If she has discerned in him the qualities of a husband, she is free to say yes. If she does not feel she has adequate base to discern whether she could pursue making covenant with him, she needs to ask for more time.

The issue is not making a rigid law of how this is to take place. The objective of courtship is protecting the man and woman from anything that could hurt them and destroy their destiny. To do so, certain precautions are established to guide them into the destination of God's desire.

After a period of courting that is determined by each individual situation, the couple enters into engagement if all parties are in agreement. As you can see, courtship brings all jurisdictions of godly government into the process of decision making. Individual government, family government and church government all work together to discern and confirm the Lord's will in who He joins. In doing so, it provides a firm foundation upon which a Kingdom marriage can be built.

Living By Divine Decree

This list of Destiny Destroyers has not been designed to be an exhaustive list. We could also develop such issues as compromise, sin, unforgiveness, unresolved conflict and unconfessed past issues, etc. These and others can become spiritual time bombs the enemy uses to pull out and use against us when we have reached our maximum level of spiritual usefulness. Our challenge is to resolve them now, so the Holy Spirit can be free to guide us into our predetermined destiny.

Destiny is a spiritual inheritance. It must be sought, it must be protected. As we seek first the Kingdom of God, keeping our eyes wholly on the person of Jesus Christ, we can walk in the assurance of God's direction and the fulfillment it brings. We can live in the confidence that our children will be raised in the godly admonition of the Lord. As we train them in the way they should go, we can be assured that when they grow up, they will not depart from that way.

FOOTNOTES:

14. Matthew 10:39
15. Philippians 3:10
16. II Corinthians 3:18
17. II Timothy 2:14
18. I Corinthians 15:33

The SILENCE
of the LAMBS

A Call to Fathers

Silence may be golden in Hollywood, but in the family it can be deadly. From the time of Adam right up to the present day, Satan has deployed a strategy of forgetfulness and silence to render the man ineffective in his mandate to rule and subdue the earth. Man forgets who he is and, as a result, remains silent in the face of dominion.

"I looked for a man among them who would build up the wall and stand before me in the gap on behalf of the land so I would not have to destroy it, but I found none." *(Ezekiel 22:30)*

This verse has got to be one of the most tragic verses in all of Scripture. It is a verse that reveals both the desire and the disappointment of God when His desire was not realized.

God is not a sexist. He does not place a greater value on the man than He does the woman. In regard to the value and worth we stand equal, but in regard to function, God's selection is evident. He has placed the mantle of leadership and headship on the man. Fathers are to take the government role of leadership when it comes to the training of the generations to come. This does not mean that mothers are not to take a vital role, for they most certainly do. Mothers are to impart the feminine nature of God and fathers the masculine. When both are imparted together, the child is nurtured in a healthy and godly environment.

A New Hour For Men

Father is, without question, bringing the focus of His attention to bear on men these past few years. The organization for men, *Promise Keepers*, was "Exhibit A" of God's desire. Who would have ever imagined that we would see the vast number of men coming to these events in every major city in our land? The good news is, not only is God speaking to men, but men are responding as never before. As we men respond, the Holy Spirit is awakening us to be aware of the demonic strategy of forgetfulness and silence.

Thiefology

Theology is the science and study of God.[19] It is the understanding that God follows a systematic pattern of behavior that is definable and consistent.

Similarly, to coin a word, thiefology would be defined as the science and study of Satan. I am not suggesting we study his ways to focus on him or give him any undue attention, but if we are going to enforce the victory of Calvary in our everyday lives, we must become wise to his strategy in order not to fall prey to his tactics.

Strategy is the plan or scheme devised to defeat an enemy. Tactics are the actions devised to execute the plan. So if the strategy were to eliminate troop movement, the tactic would be to blow up the bridge. If the strategy were to cut off communications, the tactic would be to eliminate the telephone and satellites.

From the beginning, Satan's strategy has been to eliminate mankind from dominion of the earth. (Genesis 1:26-29) In various portions of Scripture we find him executing a few tactics over and over. In Genesis 3, it was the tactic of doubt. In Numbers 16, it was the tactic of insurrection and disloyalty. In the book of Judges, the tactic was independence and an unwillingness to be led. In II Samuel 11, the tactic was lust and adultery. In I Corinthians 10, it was a tactic of gossip and grumbling. Throughout the Word of God, we can see the pattern of these tactics working its carnage and leaving the church ineffective in the battle. The problem is that many of these tactics have become acceptable in the church. Though the Word of God takes an aggressive stand against gossip and slander, it is now accepted by most as a normal part of everyday life. This ought not to be.

THIEFOLOGY IN THE HOME

Satan's strategy for the home has been to eliminate man from the role of headship in his family, thereby making Christianity primarily a woman's religion. Two of Satan's tactics to accomplish this have been forgetfulness and silence. Genesis 3:1-7 is the account of Satan's first strike with man.

SATAN'S STRATEGY WAS TWOFOLD

1. Break man's fellowship with God and thereby thwart dominion.

2. Eliminate the man's active role in the family and thereby thwart his headship.

Satan's Tactic to Enact His Strategy was also Twofold

1. Break man's fellowship through forgetfulness - when we sin we must forget who we are.

 2. Eliminate man's active role through silence -you need not eliminate man's physical presence if you can take his voice.

Jesus taught us that the Kingdom of God is an indirect Kingdom. So to save our lives, we must first lose them. *(Luke 9:24)* To be first, we must be last. *(Mark 9:35)* If we seek after everything we will lose it, but if we seek the Kingdom of God first and His righteousness, everything will be added to us. *(Matthew 6:33)*

Understanding that Lucifer was trained under the hand of God, we know he follows an indirect pattern. As God's plan is unfolded little by little, so Satan's plan is a pattern of subtle conditioning, step by step, little by little, sowing his seeds of destruction. He need not take the man out of the home, if he can render him ineffective through forgetfulness and silence. He need not take the wife and children, if he can make the man too busy to notice them.

The Tactic of Forgetfulness

"Did God really say?..." (Genesis 3:1)

Though Satan addressed the woman, by virtue of God's mandate to man, Adam should have answered for Eve. God commanded Adam to rule over the beasts of the field *(Genesis 1:28)*, not receive instructions from them. But Adam forgot who he was. He forgot what his commission was and he allowed the serpent to speak to his wife, leaving her unprotected from temptation.

The serpent's twofold strategy with Adam and Eve in Genesis 3 was:

1. Question God's directive, thereby causing doubt. *"You must not eat from any tree."* (3:1)

2. Redefine the directive, thereby causing forgetfulness in Adam and Eve. *"For God knows that when you eat of it your eyes will be opened and you will be like God."* (3:5)

A Sower of Doubt; A Master of Redefinition

> Is it really wrong? After all everybody is doing it. God just doesn't want you to have fun."

> "Johnny didn't do anything really bad. Kids will be kids you know. After all, we are under grace. So don't use the rod, he may think he is being abused."

> How will you know if you really love him if you don't date him for awhile. Go ahead. Give him your heart; you have nothing to lose. If it doesn't work out, you can just try again."

Satan is a master at redefining words and intent. Time and time again I have seen the ground of truth lost because he has redefined a word and surrounded it in controversy. Once the word is surrounded in controversy, we are afraid to do it. He redefines the rod with abuse, and then many are afraid to use it, in spite of the biblical command. He redefines submission as chauvinism, so many are unwilling to extend it in spite of Ephesians five. Discipleship, shepherding, Kingdom—all biblical words that have been redefined and are now the focal point of controversy. Once the redefined word is accepted, the old definition of the word is removed, its practice is forgotten.

The Beginning of the End

The fall of man began by Adam forgetting who he was and what it was Father had commissioned him to do. He was commissioned to rule and subdue the serpent, not to listen to and follow. Spiritual warfare is designed to cause us to forget. We forget our commission, we forget our role, we forget our calling, we forget our distinctives, and we forget our power and then we begin living as a commoner. Careers and earthly pursuits now become primary and Kingdom pursuits lag behind as secondary. Our passion for Christ becomes lukewarm and our headship in the home diminishes to a title. We begin to merely accommodate our family rather than lead them and adopt a "peace at any price" mentality. All this because we forget who we are and for what it was we were commissioned to do.

To commit adultery, you must forget who you are. You must forget that you are dead to sin. That's what happened to King David. He forgot he was a warrior. When all other warriors were at war he stayed home. One evening from his rooftop, he spied Bathsheba bathing. In the heat of that temptation he forgot he was a warrior; he forgot he was a king; he forgot he was a man after God's own heart; and he forgot he had plenty of other wives.

Understanding Satan's strategy and man's propensity to sin, God warned his people continually not to forget.

> *"Be careful not to forget the covenant of the Lord your God..."* *(Deuteronomy 4:23)*

> *"Be careful that you do not forget the Lord..."* *(Deuteronomy 6:12)*

> *"Only be careful and watch yourselves closely so that you do not forget the things your eyes have seen or let them slip from your heart as long as you live. Teach them to your children and to their children after them."* *(Deuteronomy 4:9)*

Forgetfulness is an enemy of generational transfer. In light of our responsibility to those who will come after us, we must remember who we are and what God has commissioned us to do.

A STRATEGY OF HIS OWN

Nothing catches God by surprise. He had a strategy of His own that would thwart Satan's plan. Into the very identity of man, God framed how we can be the ones who remember and then tell the story.

The Hebrew language has six words that the English language interprets as man. According to Roberts Hicks and his book, *The Masculine Journey*,[20] these six words reveal six stages man passes through in his physical and spiritual development. One of the words interpreted as man is the word "Zakar." The root meaning is to "remember, recall or retell the story."[21] Foreseeing Satan's tactic of forgetfulness, Father fashioned into the very being of man's name and identity the responsibility to remember and tell the story. Every time man heard his name "Zakar," he would be reminded that he was to remember and tell the story. As men we must constantly remember who we are. The very nature of the war we are in is designed to cause us to forget. We must remember we are to lead our families by ruling, protecting, sowing and caring. We must remember the priority to seek the Kingdom of God first. We must remember to romance our wife, invest in our children and carry a zeal for the house of God.

The Tactic of Silence

"When the woman saw that the fruit of the tree was good for food and pleasing to the eye... she took some and ate it. She also gave some to her husband, who was with her." (Genesis 3:6)

I am told the Hebrew word used for *with her* in this verse is the same word used to describe an intimate union. The picture we get from this word is the fact that Adam was closely involved with Eve throughout her discourse with the serpent and apparently never said a thing. This means the very man that was given the mandate to rule over every living creature that moves on the ground was now allowing this creature to redefine God's directive to man and now was not saying a word in defense. Adam forgot who he was and, in his forgetfulness, he remained silent.

For some reason, I had never put Adam in the same vicinity as Eve during the temptation. I am sure, subconsciously, I wanted him to be in some other place, so the blame could be squarely on the woman. But such is not the case. Adam was there, but though present, he remained silent.

It is not only what went into Adam's mouth that caused the fall; it is what did not come out of his mouth. Not only was it Adam's eating, it was his silence. The true sin of the fall was the fact that though Adam was with Eve during the temptation, he said nothing. He forgot who he was and left his wife uncovered and unprotected from temptation.

Thiefology Revisited

Thousands of years later this same tactic of silence still plagues the man of God. In the face of temptation or spiritual leadership, man's tendency is to forget who he is and thus lose his voice. Rather than telling the story, he remains silent. After many years of marital counseling, I am convinced that eighty percent of all marital problems stem from the man's silence and his lack of communication. We mask it by using terms like *unreconcilable differences.* But any difference is reconcilable if we will just talk about it and allow the Lord to make the necessary adjustment.

In defense of their silence, men often say, "Well I'm just the silent type." That could very well be true, but it is only because they have forgotten who they are. One thing for sure, they were not silent when they first met their wife and began to court her. Knowing that he would have to win his woman, this silent type of a man came out of silence (he remembered who he was!) and worked to win his woman's heart and affections. To win her, he retrained his communication habits and told her the story. He became the real man he was meant to be and it worked. He won his woman. But little by little over time, he forgot and reverted back to his cave of silence. The problem is a man never wins his woman, he just wins her over and over again. A father never wins his children, he must wins them over and over again. I once saw a bumper sticker that read, "It used to be wine, women and song; now it's beer, TV and the old lady." That is the terrible result of someone who has forgotten.

Men: Father God is desirous of reminding us who He created us to be. He is desirous of giving us our voices back. He wants to put an end to the conspiracy of forgetfulness and silence.

THE SOUNDS OF SILENCE

The sounds of man's silence may take on many different forms. Allow me to list a few:

1. Absenteeism

Though man is home, he is always absent. Perhaps it is his career that has his focus or it is his sports, hobbies and recreational pursuits. Whatever the focus, it robs the man of his godly influence in the home, especially in the formative years of his children's lives. It is during these formative years that the foundation of generational transfer is laid. As men, we cannot leave this responsibility to our wives in hopes that they will do it all. Deuteronomy 6 and Psalm 78 place the responsibility on the fathers.

2. Spiritual Dullness

How easy it is for men to be passionate about their jobs and sports, but somewhat complacent about the things of God. Though they get fanatical at their favorite sporting event, you will never find them fanatical about Jesus. For some reason they have rationalized it to be acceptable to be a sports fanatic, but not acceptable to be a Jesus fanatic. *"From the days of John the Baptist until now, the Kingdom of Heaven has been forcefully advancing and forceful men lay hold of it." (Matthew 11:12)* A faithful man is nothing more than a forceful man.

The problem is when the woman sets the spiritual pace and atmosphere in the home, the children very easily believe Christianity to be primarily a women's thing. Without the male influence, the Kingdom of God has a matriarchal tone and is consequently misrepresented.

3. Separate Lifestyles

When the man remains silent, the wife and children seek to satisfy their needs elsewhere. The worst case scenario would find them satisfying their need in some illegal manner. But far more prevalent is the wife and children finding their fulfillment and affirmation in pursuits outside and separate from the family. Not that these pursuits are necessarily wrong; it is just that they are a poor substitute for the fulfillment and protection that only a father can provide.

My Personal Testimony

I am deeply indebted to a fellow pastor and good friend named, Lon Stokes, who pastors a church in Othello, Washington. Much of what is in this chapter came from a men's retreat where Pastor Lon shared with our men at Christ Church Kirkland. During this retreat, Father began the process of giving me back my voice.

Over the weekend I became deeply convicted of the truth of my forgetfulness and silence. It was not a conviction that left me discouraged, but one that left me excited to restore my God-given identity to begin to tell the story to my family. The problem was I had set some pretty deep habit patterns of laziness that had to be ploughed up.

My journey back began with three simple practices:

I. Writing Notes

Knowing that Marcy was interested in my day and what had transpired during the day, it would take me writing periodic notes to assure my remembrance when I came home. All too often I had come home to the question "How was your day?" On any normal day my answer was, "Great!" On a talkative day my answer was "Really great!" It wasn't that I didn't want to tell her what happened; it was that I couldn't remember all that went on, especially the detail of conversations and counseling sessions. But I had this unique ability to condense a three-hour meeting into a three-word description. To overcome my forgetfulness I began jotting down notes of reminders. When I got home I could take out my note pad and describe my day in the detail that Marcy desired.

2. Managing Time

The second thing I began to do was to sit with Marcy and my children on a regular basis to go over the schedule in order to protect their time. One of the God-given needs of a woman is her need to be protected by her man. One of the ways we protect them is by giving them perspective in time management. Women tend to be far more subjective than men are, so it is much more difficult for them to say no. As the head of our family, I need-ed to step in and be a voice of protection and perspective. This is true of teenagers as well, especially teenage daughters who are pressed by the demands of friends, schoolwork, baby-sitting and everything else that presses for their time.

3. Prayer

Thirdly, I was led to lay hands on Marcy and pray for her every morning that I possibly could. I had always prayed for her and the children on a reg-ular basis, but this praying was an actual prayer in her presence. I was amazed how difficult this step became and how difficult it is to remain consistent. I am sure the difficulty of the action is in direct proportion to the effectiveness of the prayer, for the fervent prayer of a righteous man does avail much. *(James 5:16)*

As I began to do these things, I noticed Marcy began to open up like a flower to me. The more I gave myself to her, the more she gave in return.

The more I spoke to her, the softer she became to me. The more I was willing to take leadership, the more she was willing to issue submission. The more I was willing to protect, the more she was willing to follow.

RESULTS OF SILENCE

Let me share with you what this tactic of the enemy to silence husbands does to our wives.

1. Silence leaves our wives unprotected.
"Now the serpent was more crafty than any of the wild animals the Lord God had made. He said to the woman, 'Did God really say you must not eat from any tree in the garden?'" (Genesis 3:1)
Would the outcome have been different if Adam would have spoken up here and protected his wife from the serpent's temptation? In Adam's silence, he left his wife alone to defend the command God had given to him. The command not to eat of the tree was given to Adam before Eve was even formed. *(Genesis 2:17)* Even though Eve had only heard the command second hand, Adam's silence left her alone to defend the truth.

2. Silence forces our wives to chase and pursue us rather than us leading and pursuing them.
There is no question that Scripture teaches that the man is to be the leader in the marital relationship. According to I Peter 3:7, God made woman the weaker partner. She is not weaker in regard to worth or value, but in regard to leadership and initiative. It is upon the man that God places the responsibility of leadership and pursuit. The man is to be the aggressor and the one who draws his wife out. It is upon the fathers that God places the primary responsibility to draw destiny out of their children.

3. Silence forces our wives to be the "Zakar," the one who remembers and tells the story.
She plays the man's role while her man remains silent. This does not mean that the wife does not have a story of her own to tell. It is simply a definition of primary responsibility that belongs to the man. *"He commanded our forefathers to teach their children, so the next generation would know them..."* *(Psalm 78:5-6)*

4. Silence denies the woman's God-given need for communication.

Father made most women with a need for meaningful words. Unlike the man, she needs meaningful conversation and much communication. If wives do not receive meaningful conversation from their husband, they are left susceptible to temptation and the possibility of getting it from someone else.

A Strategy of Defeat

Having laid out the strategic intent and tactics of the enemy, let us look at God's strategy of defeat. What are the tactics Father employs to counteract the strategy and reverse the enemy's tactics?

I. Remember

"Remember (Zakar) this, fix it in mind, take it to heart..." (Isaiah 46:8) As men we must continually remind ourselves who we are and what our God-given responsibilities are as head of the home.

One of the ways we remember is by establishing memorials that fix these responsibilities in our minds. Here are some suggestions:

A. Assume the responsibility of putting your children to bed at night. *(Deuteronomy 6:7)* This is our opportunity as Dads to filter through our children's day and sort out issues of falsehood and difficulty. If hurtful things were said at school, we can reverse the damage. During this time we can read them the Word, pray over them and speak to them concerning their destiny and purpose in Christ.

B. Set a regular time with each of your children for just them and you. As I have mentioned, ever since my children have been in school, I have had regular breakfast time with each of them. Monday morning is Kelsey's time. Tuesday morning is Kaleb's and Wednesday morning is Kyle's. During this time we always go out for breakfast and talk. It is during times like this that discipling takes place. It is during this time that I am able to impart my heart and train them in our family distinctives. It is during this time that I have an opportunity to listen to them. By just listening, I am able to get the pulse of where they are and determine what they currently need to navigate the waters they are in.

C. Set a regular time with your spouse. The best gift a father can give his children is an example of love for his wife. One of the most meaningful transfers we give the generations to come is a fresh and vital love, husband to wife. Courtship after marriage is a fundamental principle that needs to transfer to every young man and woman. To do so we must establish a regular "Date Night" where the husband and wife get out to keep their love and appreciation for each other alive and fresh.

D. Fix a constant devotional life. Children learn more by what they see than what they hear. They can hear you talk about intimacy and devotion, but if they never see you seeking God in prayer and Bible study, it will just be words to them. Early rising is a biblical practice that needs to be practiced in the home. Our children need to see us conquer our love for the bed and offer the first fruits of our day to Jesus. Perhaps you pray on your way to work or do your Bible study after your children have left for school. All that is well and good, but if we desire generational transfer, our children need to see us practicing what we are desirous of them emulating.

2. Pursue

"The Kingdom of Heaven has been forcefully advancing, and forceful men lay hold of it." (Matthew 11:12) Spiritual inactivity and passivity is a stronghold of our day. Due to the compromised standard of modernity, our message has not called most people to action. Consequently, inactivity has been the norm. A gospel that just calls us to action on Sunday mornings and Wednesday nights is not the gospel of the Kingdom of God. The gospel of the Kingdom is a gospel of action. It is a gospel of pursuit. It is a gospel that is in constant advance, and it calls those who follow it to advance with it. Jesus Christ died a radical death so that we might have a radical life that is a spent in radical pursuit of the Kingdom of God and its purpose in our lives.

The principles of the tithe can be applied to the stewarding of our whole lives, not just our money. Even as God owns all our income, He asks only for ten percent though He owns our entire lives. We must acknowledge His ownership in our lives by giving Him the proper time needed to pursue Him with all our might.

For the sake of the generations to come, we must leave them an example of radical pursuit. Our sons and daughters must see us more passionate about the Kingdom than we are about anything in this world. Understanding that more is caught than is taught, they will receive more by us leaving an example of aggressive pursuit.

Aggressive pursuit of the Kingdom is best exemplified in a life of personal devotion and daily obedience to Christ. For true generational transfer to transpire, our sons and daughters must see our pursuit of God in regular prayer and study of the Word. For them to catch the vision of radical pursuit, they must first see it. They must see our daily choices to obey the call of God in our lives, regardless of the personal cost. As they see us taking up our cross and following Christ daily, an indelible example will be written on their minds and in their spirits. We must continually guard our relationship to the Lord from becoming utilitarian. Our relationship to Him must be deeper than just our sense of need. Yes, we must come to Him not only out of our need, but ever more importantly, out of love for Him.

3. Speech

"Those who feared the Lord talked with each other… A scroll of remembrance was written…" (Malachi 3:16) Getting our voices back and securing a successful generational transfer begins with remembrance. We must remember, as men, that the very foundation of our identity is to remember and tell the story. Malachi encourages both of these identity traits. Those who feared the Lord *talked* and it was all *recorded* in a scroll of remembrance.

For the sake of a successful generational transfer, we must train ourselves to come out of our silence and speak. Our silence has become a learned response. Though we think it to be quite natural, it is not according to our created design. God designed us to be those who would tell the story. Telling the story requires us retraining ourselves to come out of patterns of silence. As husbands, we must speak to our wives about our day and ask them about theirs. Speaking to them involves more than just a mere rehearsal of the facts. We must learn to share our feelings along with the facts. This will require a level of vulnerability that most men are not accoustomed to, but nevertheless, are in need of learning. We must learn to speak to our wives words of romance and tenderness.

We must speak to the spiritual atmosphere in our homes. We do so by making worship and prayer a normal aspect of our daily living. We should be those who make singing and praying a normal aspect of our daily experience. The corporate dynamic of worship and prayer was never intended to replace the personal song of our lips of continual prayer. As our children see our example of worship and prayer in our homes, they will grow accustomed to that being the normal Christian life.

We must learn to speak to our children concerning their destinies. Our children belong to God and are placed in our care as a stewardship. Therefore, we must seek the Lord in order to discern His intention for those He has placed in our care. As we gain a clear sense of the purpose God has for them, we must speak prophetically to that end, clearly describing to them the destiny we sense from the Lord. We must speak to them concerning the call of God and the mandate to follow. We must speak words of encouragement and faith in order to inspire expectation within them to rise up and so fulfill their destiny. We must speak to their need to make wise decisions that will facilitate their destiny, not thwart it. For the sake of generational transfer, we must not be afraid to lead even when it means saying *no*. In fact, *no* should be our answer to any decision, relationship or direction that is not in direct harmony with the destiny God has revealed for them. God chose Abraham because He knew Abraham would command his children. *(Genesis 18:19)* We must be willing to walk in the footsteps of our father, Abraham. Commanding them means training them to make the difficult decisions and learning the value of saying *no*.

STEP BY STEP

Generational transfer is a process, not an event. The success of generational transfer is directly tied to the step-by step process laid out through the years. It does not begin at eighteen years of age, but at birth, and it takes daily practice. It is those daily consistencies seen in our example that sets the course for our children to follow and reinforces their desire to continue in the way of their fathers. Absentee fathers have been the curse of generational transfer. Let us remember who we are as men and begin once again to tell the story of God's goodness and the wonder of His matchless grace.

FOOTNOTES:

19. Webster's Dictionary
20. Roberts Hicks, The Masculine Journey. (It is my understanding that Robert Hicks Masculine Journey has come under considerable scrutiny as to its Biblical accuracy. It is not my intent to support the position or deny it. The intent is simply to underscore the importance of every believer growing from child to reproducer. Whether Hicks position is an accurate support for this is open for discussion, but what is clear is the need to reproduce the life of Christ in us, in order for the process of generational transfer to occur.)
21. Strong's Concordance

SINS *of the* FATHERS

Sins of the Fathers

The truth of generational transfer is like a door that swings both ways. Just as truth is passed through the generational lines, so is sin. Sinful habits and their resulting curses that are not brought under the blood of Jesus Christ stand the risk of being passed on through the generational line.

Freedom from the Ancient Ruins

"They will rebuild the ancient ruins and restore the places long devastated; they will renew the ruined cities that have been devastated for generations." (Isaiah 61:4)

Please note the time frame in the above passage. The freedom promised is freedom from the *"ancient"* ruins, the places *"long"* devastated, and the cities devastated for *"generations."* As we travel this ancient path of generational transfer, we inevitably discover some ancient ruins that have been in our family line for generations. These are the sins in our life that are not the direct result of our sowing and reaping, but rather, sins we have inherited through our generational line.

A generational evaluation of sin deals with sin from its root cause. Sin has both its root and its fruit. The root is the cause; the fruit is the result. This chapter deals with sin from its root.

Management or Elimination

As society rejects the law Word of God, it also rejects the very means of its freedom and healing. As the Word of God is rejected, society must come up with alternative explanations and ways to manage the consequences of its sin. The Word of God states very clearly that Jesus is our payment for sin *(Romans 6:23)*, but when that Word is rejected, man is left to manage his sin rather than experience freedom from it. Alternative explanations redefine sins as weaknesses. Choices that lead to death are described as diseases. Reaping of sin's consequences are redefined as chemical imbalances and hormonal deficiencies. (This is not to say there are not valid cases of chemical imbalances and hormonal deficiencies.) Those who dare call these behaviors sin are actually labeled as intolerant oppressors and, in some cases, are labeled as responsible for the emotional state the victim is in.

wow

The problem with this new redefinition is when sinful behavior is no longer labeled as sin, the road to deliverance is impossible. In the redefinition, deliverance is substituted for management. However, sin is incredibly difficult to manage. When our sinful behavior is defined by the standard of God's Word deliverance is not only possible, but it is swift in the face of repentance. The blood of Jesus Christ covers our sin and His cross delivers us from it. His blood shed on the cross is designed to deal with fictitious diseases or redefined imbalances. It is cruel to redefine sin and relegate one to a lifetime of management, when the blood of Jesus Christ promises immediate deliverance from sin. *Wow!* *His power!*

A Sinful Inheritance

All of us come into life carrying baggage. King David said it this way, *"Surely I have been a sinner from birth, sinful from the time my mother conceived me." (Psalm 51:5)* This sinful inheritance predisposes us to certain mindsets and behaviors that are in need of reconstruction. All of us come into life with certain issues that have been in our family line for generations. These issues are the ancient ruins. These are the patterns that have been passed down through the generations and have left particular areas in the family long devastated.

These perhaps could be patterns of self-pity, greed, anger, alcoholism, chemical dependency, depression, rejection, unfaithfulness, control, and poverty, etc. Marcy and I recently prayed with a young lady struggling with drunkenness. Twenty years ago we ministered to this young lady's father for the same sin. Hers is a case of generational sin, not an inherited disease. Oh, it is most definitely inherited, but it is inherited sin, not a disease.

"You shall not make for yourself an idol in the form of anything in heaven above or on the earth beneath or in the waters below. You shall not bow down to them or worship them; for I, the Lord your God, am a jealous God, punishing the children for the sin of the fathers to the third and fourth generation of those who hate me, but showing love to a thousand generations of those who love me and keep my commandments." (Exodus 20:4-6)

The western mind has come to view man very individualistically. It sees man as an individual responsible only for himself. This is not how God thinks. God views man in terms of families. God thinks in terms of generations. No man sins unto himself. When one leaves his or her sins uncovered, those sins are passed on to the coming generations. We are deeply affected by our parents' sins, if we do not bring those sins under the blood of Christ and appropriate His completed work. Inheriting the sins of our fathers does not force us to repeat the sin or leave us without a choice. We sin only if we *choose* to sin, but the generational influence does put added pressure on us in the particular area that was not dealt with. We need not accept this generational transfer of sin, for Jesus Christ cancelled the written code giving generational sin access to us. We become subject to the transfer only if we choose to enter into our parents' sinful way and not appropriate Christ's completed work.

BIBLICAL EXAMPLES OF GENERATIONAL SIN

Perhaps the clearest example of generational sin in the Bible is King David and his generations that followed. As we read of King David in I & II Samuel and I Kings, we see that he was a man after God's heart that experienced a tremendous number of victories. Soon after his sin with Bathsheba, his life began to crumble. King David fell into the sins of adultery (*II Samuel 11:4*), deception (*II Samuel 11:8*), conspiracy (*II Samuel 11:14-15*) and murder (*II Samuel 11:16-17*).

David was most definitely forgiven for each of these sins, but his forgiveness did not prevent those sins of the fathers and their resulting curses from being passed onto to his family life. Forgiveness does not stop the curse. The cross stops the curse only when it is appropriated.[22] After David's transgression, he repented and prayed the great prayer of repentance found in Psalm 51. Later, we read of the impact David's sin had on his following generations. Amnon, one of David's sons raped Tamar[23] which led to Amnon being murdered by another of David's sons, Absalom.[24] The same deception, lying and conspiracy contained in David's sins are also found in his sons. The story of this generational sin ends with Absalom's rebellion and subsequent death.

Another example is of Abraham and Isaac. Both he and his son were guilty of lying,[25] saying their wives were their sisters. Rebekah lied to Isaac about her two sons and even called for the resulting curse to be upon her.[26] Likewise, Jacob was guilty of lying and deceiving throughout his whole life. Jacob's wife Rachel stole her father's household gods and lied about them. This resulted in Jacob's unintentional curse, which resulted in her early death.[27] While the blessing of generational transfer far outweighs the curse, it is clear that the sins of the fathers are passed on through the family line. In Christ, we suffer for our father's sins only if we choose to remain in the sinful way. If we redefine them as diseases or imbalances, when they are in reality sin, we are doomed to a lifetime of management when deliverance is our inheritance in Christ.

FREEDOM FROM GENERATIONAL SIN

1. Confess.

Freedom from the sins of our fathers begins with confession.

"But if they will confess their sins and the sins of their fathers—their treachery against me and their hostility toward me, which made me hostile toward them so that I sent them into the land of their enemies—then when their uncircumcised hearts are humbled and they pay for their sin, I will remember my covenant with Jacob and my covenant with Isaac and my covenant with Abraham, and I will remember the land." (Leviticus 26:40-42)

Please note that this passage does not require us to take responsibility for our forefather's sins, but to acknowledge them and confess them. It does require us to take responsibility for our subsequent action that may have resulted from our forefather's sin.

2. Appropriate.

Once we have confessed the sins of our fathers, we must appropriate the cross. *"All who rely on observing the law are under a curse, for it is written: 'Cursed is everyone who does not continue to do everything written in the Book of the Law.' Clearly no one is justified before God by the law, because, 'The righteous will live by faith.' The law is not based on faith; on the contrary, 'The man who does these things will live by them.' Christ redeemed us from the curse of the law by becoming a curse for us, for it is written: 'Cursed is everyone who is hung on a tree.' He redeemed us in order that the blessing given to Abraham might come to the Gentiles through Christ Jesus, so that by faith we might receive the promise of the Spirit. (Galatians 3:10-14)*

THE APOSTLE PETER FURTHER ILLUSTRATES THIS:

"For you know that it was not with perishable things such as silver or gold that you were redeemed from the empty way of life handed down to you from your forefathers, but with the precious blood of Christ, a lamb without blemish or defect." (I Peter 1:18-19)

Appropriation is simply the act of applying the truth of God's Word to whatever your situation might be. To appropriate the cross to generational sin is to pray a prayer of application that applies the completed work of Christ on the cross to the generational pattern of your family line.

3. Repent.

Following confession and appropriation, we repent from any involvement of the sin we may have entered into. We must repent from this sin and turn the other way.

4. Renounce.

After repentance, we must make a verbal break from the pattern we once followed and renounce any allegiance to the sinful family way.

5. Break. *once broken always broken.*

Once we have renounced the former way, we must make a verbal break of any tie to the family way. We must break the power of any curse resulting from the sinful way by bringing it under the authority of Jesus Christ.

6. Receive.

The result of all this is that we must receive full and complete forgiveness, knowing that Jesus Christ is faithful and just to forgive us of all sins, even the sins of our forefathers.

NEW CREATIONS IN CHRIST

"Therefore, if anyone is in Christ, he is a new creation; the old has gone, the new has come!" (II Corinthians 5:17)

In Christ we are new creations with a new inheritance. The inheritance of our forefathers is cancelled and we are free to walk in the newness of our relationship to Christ. Jesus Christ sets us on new ground making way for the purity of generational transfer without the baggage of our former life.

FOOTNOTES:

22. II Samuel 13:1-18
23. II Samuel 13:28-29
24. Genesis 20:2; 26:7
25. Genesis 27:12-13
26. Genesis 35:16-20

live as a victor not victim.

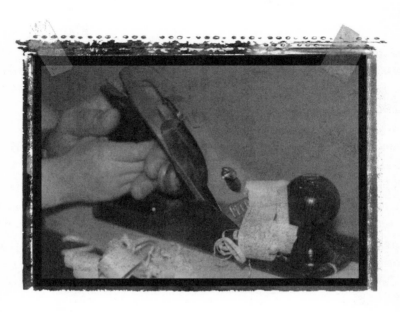

DAD *to the* BONE

Exercising a Will to Rule

Fathers play the key role in the transfer of truth. As we look to the ancient path of generational transfer, we find that it was the fathers who were commanded to blaze the trail. It was the fathers who were designed by God to "tell the story."

"I will open my mouth in parables, I will utter hidden things, things from of old—what we have heard and known, what our fathers have told us. We will not hide them from their children; we will tell the next generation the praiseworthy deeds of the Lord, His power, and the wonders He has done. He decreed statutes for Jacob and established the law in Israel, which He commanded our forefathers to teach their children, so the next generation would know them, even the children yet to be born, and they in turn would tell their children. Then they would put their trust in God and would not forget His deeds but would keep His commands." (Psalm 78:2-7)

The ancient struggle of every believer throughout time has been the willingness to do what they know. The fact that we know something and thoroughly understand it does not guarantee we will walk in it. James makes this quite clear when he admonishes us to not be hearers of the Word only, but to be doers *(James 1:22)*.

Amen

Our point of accountability is not the mind, but the will. Our lack of obedience is not a knowledge problem, but a will problem. To know to do right and not do it reveals an unbroken will. We must continually place ourselves before the Lord and cry out for His grace that makes us *"to will and to do of His good pleasure." (Philippians 2:13)*

A Will to Rule

"Then God said, 'Let us make man in our image, in our likeness, and let them rule over the fish of the sea and the birds of the air, over the livestock, over all the earth, and over all the creatures that move along the ground.' So God created man in his own image, in the image of God He created him; male and female He created them. God blessed them and said to them, 'Be fruitful and increase in number; fill the earth and subdue it. Rule over the fish of the sea and the birds of the air and over every living creature that moves on the ground.'" (Genesis 1:26-28)

Man's original commission from God was a commission to rule. He charged Adam to fill the earth and rule over it. He was to rule his family and be God's representative to those who would follow after him. Man's rule was not a self-appointed rule or an arbitrary rule, but a representative rule. Please note that man was created in the image of God *before* He was given the commission to rule. Consequently, as an image bearer, his type of rule was to be the exact image of how God rules. He was to rule graciously, and lovingly. *good*

In the commission to rule, God designed a fellowship. Relationship with God is both established and deepened through the fellowship of labor. In work, we are able to discover more of the character and nature of God. The Apostle Paul picks this concept up in Ephesians 2 when he says, *"For we are God's workmanship, created in Christ Jesus to do good works, which God prepared in advance for us to do." (Ephesians 2:10)* God is so committed to this fellowship of labor, He prepared work in advance for us to do.

Soon after Adam's commission to rule, he forgot both who he was and what he was called to do. Rather than ruling over the serpent, Adam received his instructions from it. As a result of his forgetfulness, man fell and that fellowship of labor was broken. In his forgetfulness, Adam lost his will to rule.

Having a will to rule brings us into fellowship with our heavenly Father. Satan's strategy from the beginning of time has been to break our fellowship with God and thereby thwart our dominion of the earth. Our dominion means Satan's eviction, so his aim is to prevent us from ruling.

Satan is a strategist. He knows that to break our fellowship directly would mean a certain all out war, which he would rather avoid, for he knows our victory is promised. Rather than going after our fellowship directly and fighting the ensuing war, he takes the indirect route and goes after our will to rule. For if he can rob us of our will to rule, he also robs us of our fellowship of labor.

help me to see + be responsible!

MAN'S FUNDAMENTAL NEED

The most fundamental need men face today is to either recapture or protect their will to rule. Most men have lost this will to rule with their wives, so they have pacified themselves with just being a figurehead authority. Yes, they may be the heads in their homes, but their wives are the necks that turn them, In the void of rule, wives have stepped in to fill the vacuum. It is not because they have some evil desire to take over, but they have stepped into the void out of the instinct to survive and preserve the family.

Most fathers have also lost their will to rule their children. They have resorted to anger or have left all discipline to the mother. The result of this forfeiture? Their wives are left unprotected and forced into a rule of their own. Consequently, children are often left to themselves and never learn the security in being cared for or the blessing of leadership.

Being a deceiver, the serpent came to the woman first. He came to the one who was not in charge. God, on the other hand, came to Adam first. He came and addressed the one He had commissioned to rule.

THE WOMAN'S URGE

"To the woman He said, … 'Your desire will be for your husband, and he will rule over you.'" (Genesis 3:16)

Keep in mind this was spoken to Eve as judgment, not blessing. The desire God speaks about here is not a righteous desire, but rather a desire to lead. The New English Bible translates this verse, *"You will be eager for your husband."* [27] This is not an eagerness to bless, but rather an ambitious eagerness to lead. The footnote for this verse in the New English Bible reads, *"You will feel an urge for your husband."* [28]

The result of Adam forfeiting his will to rule became an underlining conflict between the man and the woman, between the husband and wife. The conflict, centered in man's original commission, is: will the man rule his family and faithfully represent God? Will the woman receive the rule of her husband and keep her *"urge"* for him in check? If the woman's *"urge"* comes forth, will the man have enough of the original commission in him to stand his ground and point his wife back to the Lord without losing his Christ-likeness and resorting to chauvinism?

RULING LIKE CHRIST

Ruling is not controlling or manipulating to get one's way. To co-rule with Jesus is to rule like Jesus. Ruling like Jesus is not chauvinism, nor is it superiority. To rule like Jesus rules is to serve our families, to protect them,

THE *Ancient* PATH [II]

and to lay down our lives for our families as Christ did for the church.

"And Adam was not the one deceived; it was the woman who was deceived and became a sinner." (I Timothy 2:14)

Adam's sin was the sin of abdication and passivity. Eve's sin was the sin of deception. Because of woman's propensity to temptation, her man must be willing to rule by being a spiritual covering for her and not accommodating her. An accommodating husband not only loses his fellowship of labor with God, he also loses the respect of his wife. It is very difficult for a woman to submit to a man whom she does not respect. The key to respect is a man living a respectable life, conducting himself by a standard that commands respect. He is to be an example. After all, he is God's representative in the home. To be a representative is to *re-present* what has already been presented. To represent God requires a lifestyle of devotion, service, sensitivity, leadership and godly pursuit. A godly man will seek to influence rather than control.

Where there is no will to rule, a man will resort to accommodation. He will accommodate his wife and accommodate his children. His motto becomes, "peace at any price." Webster defines accommodation as, "something supplied for convenience." But ruling is seldom convenient. Ruling means making the tough decisions. Ruling means learning to say no. It is time consuming and unpopular, but it is very necessary.

A second definition by Webster for accommodation is "to grant a loan without security." When as men we accommodate our wives or children, we leave them without security. Accommodation is not investing in our family's life but it is taking a loan from them without offering them security.

When there is no will to rule, there is no government, no peace and no fear of God. Consequently, our families become insecure. God has created women with a basic need for security. When this need of security is not met by the godly rule of her husband, she often resorts to self-rule and that urge for her husband becomes a driving force to lead.

A Description of Godly Rule

To best describe what godly rule looks like, let me simply give an expanded definition of the word "rule." Webster gives three definitions of the word "rule."

The first definition is *to exert control, direction or influence*. Ruling has progressive stages. It is through Holy Spirit discernment that we must determine what level of ruling is necessary for the circumstance or season in which we find ourselves.

Stage 1: Control

I already said that godly rule is not control. That is precisely true in relationship to fully mature adults, but in relationship to young children, control is a necessary aspect in the art of ruling. Control is the appropriate level of ruling whenever you are faced with immaturity or irresponsibility. This type of rule was necessary for the little boy I saw slugging his mother in the toy store, which I mentioned earlier.

Stage 2: Direction

As our children grow and begin to express signs of maturity and bear the fruit of sound decisions, our need for control is no longer necessary. At this stage in their lives, our ruling expresses itself in direction rather than control. Instead of making them do something, we direct them in how it is to be done. We make our will fully known and explain how they are to fulfill that will. We then allow them to do it.

Stage 3: Influence

The goal of our instruction is influence. If our rule has been successful in their lives, our influence will continue even when we are not present. Influence results in their internal restraint. Our influence becomes a law within them, enabling them to make right choices rather than being savaged by wrong decisions.

Control is designed for children. Direction is designed for youth and influence is designed for adults. These three stages are not necessarily age-related, but, they are maturity related. I have seen adults in need of being controlled (but only God is qualified to do so) and I have seen children responsible enough to be influenced, rather than controlled.

A father carries the credible influence in his family. God has programmed wives and children to be responders to that influence. When a father walks in his calling, his family responds to his position.

The influence of a father is reinforced when he does the following:

1. Becomes an example of godly pursuit.

"From the days of John the Baptist until now, the Kingdom of Heaven has been forcefully advancing, and forceful men lay hold of it." (Matthew 11:12) An ongoing complaint I receive from wives is, "My husband never spends time with the Lord." The lack of a husband's godly pursuit results in an insecure wife and a lack of trust. A wife finds a key aspect of her security from her husband's godly pursuit. As she sees him pursuing God and tastes of the fruit of that pursuit, she is able to rest secure and extend trust to her husband.

find my identity in Lord

SOME PRACTICAL SUGGESTIONS FOR A MAN'S GODLY PURSUIT:

> Let your family see you pursuing the Lord. This suggestion is not motivated out of performance. It is for the sake of example. As our families see us pursuing Him through Bible study, prayer and a continual yielding of our will to Him, they learn from our example and receive the generational transfer. Generational transfer does not take place in a vacuum. It happens because there is the demonstration of truth given, and then that demonstration is received.

> When your family asks for advice, pray. Do not just give them common sense; give them wisdom that comes from the fruit of godly pursuit.

> As you pursue God, share with your family what He is saying to you. Let them taste of the fruit and glean the benefit of a father who pursues God.

2. Becomes the family priest.

"These commandments that I give you today are to be upon your hearts. Impress them on your children. Talk about them when you sit at home and when you walk along the road, when you lie down and when you get up." (Deuteronomy 6:6-7)

As the family priests, we represent the family to God, and God to the family. We stand in the middle ground of representation. How can we present Him to our family, if we are not actively pursuing Him? *this is me—*

SOME PRACTICAL SUGGESTIONS ON BEING A FAMILY PRIEST:

> Keep your wife and children accountable to a biblical lifestyle. We must study to know the Word and lead our family into conformity to it. We must

be man enough to say *no* when God says *no* and *yes* when God says *yes*. We must be man enough to keep our families pure, especially in the areas of relationship. We must keep them free from gossip, faultfinding and other actions that destroy relationship.

> Lead your children in the way they form relationships, the way they dress and what they do for entertainment. A priest *directs,* not *suggests.* Remember you are re-presenting God to your children. You must direct them into a lifestyle pleasing to Him.

A priest will keep his children at the cross and not save them from the consequences of the sin. As parents we must never try to be nicer than Jesus, drinking their cup for them. When they are reaping the consequences of the sin, we must equip them in the process and not save them from it.

3. Gives his children a vision to live for and one worth dying for.

Your lifestyle and pursuits, not your words, are what define your children's vision. Based on your lifestyle, your children will do one of two things: either they will follow if they find your lifestyle truthful and consistent with your beliefs, or they will rebel, if they find your lifestyle hypocritical and inconsistent with your beliefs.

SOME PRACTICAL SUGGESTIONS ON GIVING YOUR CHILDREN VISION:

> Discover and walk out God's purpose for your life. When it comes to generational transfer, more is caught than is taught. As they see you walking in the fullness of Father's vision for your life, they will catch the necessity of doing the same. This means you must discover what it is you were apprehended for and walk in its fullness.

> Draw your children into your life purpose. Generational transfer sees life as a relay race, not a marathon. That is, each generation succeeds the previous one in its race, rather than each generation starting over with its own. This means Father's vision for our children's lives is inseparably tied to His vision for our own. This does not mean that they will do the exact thing you are doing, but whatever they do will be a continuation of what you have begun.

> Invest time and focus on your children. In the limitation of a child's understanding, love equals time spent. To say we love our children and not

invest time in them, is to sow confusion into their understanding for they understand love in terms of time spent with them. As they grow and mature in their understanding, they come to realize that love is much deeper than just time, but in their formative years, love equals time.

Training and discipline requires a tremendous amount of withdrawal. Consequently, there must also be sufficient amount of deposit to cover that withdrawal. Time spent with our children is one of the primary means of deposit. As we spend time with them and invest in the development of their lives, we are making a deposit into the bank of their well being. Sufficient deposit results in a relationship of wealth. An overdrawal results in rebellion.

Generational transfer is a matter of the heart. For truth to transfer from one generation to the next, we must have our children's hearts. The reason children forsake the way of their parents and choose a contrary way is because somewhere along the way parents lost their children's hearts. One of the most important ways to keep our children's hearts is to invest time with them. We must guard our lives from allowing other issues to crowd in and push our children out.

SOME PRACTICAL SUGGESTIONS ON INVESTING TIME:

> Put your children to bed at night. *"Impress them on your children… when you lie down…" (Deuteronomy 6:7)* One of the highlights of my life is the joy of putting my children to bed at night. Each time as I sit with them individually, it gives me an opportunity to filter their day, speak purpose into their life and close their day out with prayer.

> Set aside weekly time with each child alone. As I previously stated, I have a breakfast appointment each week individually with my children. This gives them their time alone with their dad when I can train them, invest in them and just love them. Use this time to teach your children to pray and hear the voice of God. Use it to speak to them about their destiny. Use it to just be with them and let them know you cherish each moment you have together.

Webster's second definition of the word "rule" is to *exert control by curbing or restraining.* A will to rule begins with having the courage to say no. No, is a word that is all but lost in many parenting practices today. A will to rule recognizes that God has a way for our children to follow and it is the fear of God that persuades me to keep my children in that way regardless of what others may be doing. A favorite motto around our home is, "Others may, but I can't." It matters little what other children are permitted to do. The only thing that truly matters is what God expects of us in the specific situation.

Paul's encouragement to Timothy is appropriate encouragement to fathers as well: *"Preach the Word; be prepared in season and out of season; correct, rebuke and encourage—with great patience and careful instruction." (II Timothy 4:2)* Ruling most certainly involves the necessity of convincing, rebuking and encouraging with great patience and careful instruction.

Parents today are very easily manipulated by their children. It seems that parents are afraid to cross their children's wills. Being afraid to cross the will of our children reveals a loss of the understanding of representative authority. Our children are not ours; they belong to God. They are given to us only as a stewardship. Because we are stewards, our primary point of accountability is God, not our children. We are responsible before God to lead our children in His way, and not to permit our children to have their own way. A child left to itself disgraces its mother.[29]

Webster's third definition of the word "rule" is to *determine and declare authoritatively.*

"You know the rulers of the Gentiles lord it over them, and their high officials exercise authority over them. Not so with you. Instead, whoever wants to become great among you must be your servant, and whoever wants to be first must be your slave." (Matthew 20:25-27)

Authoritative parenting exercises representative authority. It is a father who uses his authority to serve. He seeks to influence, not to control. Our rule in the home is never self-appointed. We represent Jesus. So we speak, determine and declare only as He speaks, determines and declares. But, when He has spoken, we must have the courage to re-present what He has stated.

Webster's fourth definition of the word "Rule" is to *govern, decide or determine judicially.* Dennis Peacocke has aptly defined the word "father" as, "He who decides." To rule in the home is to have the courage to make decisions even when those decisions may not be the popular ones. Many fathers act more like politicians than they do fathers. Their decision-making is determined by the popular vote of the family, rather than the will of God.

To govern judicially is to examine the law Word of God and make decsions accordingly. Often I hear fathers say, "They must make their own choice."

To leave our children to make their own choices may be fine and good if they were not accountable to a higher will than their own. But we must understand that they are accountable to God's destiny for their lives, and that we are accountable to lead them into that destiny. This means that we must govern our families and make judicial decisions for our children, even when it would not be their popular choice. Our children are not our own; they belong to God. God has chosen us as fathers to stand in as His representative and determine judicially whether or not our children's behavior and direction is in harmony with the Word of God. We must sow generational accountability into them early on. In doing so, they will grow up with an understanding that they are not the center of the universe, and every decision they make impacts the generation to come.

A Time For Evaluation

How deep is your commitment to generational transfer? How deep is your desire for fatherhood? A surface commitment to our children will not guarantee the transfer of truth or provide the proper insurance of our children taking the purposes of God further than we do.

We must be "Dads to the bone." Our families have been given to us as a stewardship. As stewards, we must present them back to Father with increase. To do so, we must create an atmosphere in our homes that will be conducive to spiritual growth.

Dads, you have been commissioned to rule and subdue. Rest in the security of your commission and exercise your will to rule.

Footnotes:

27. New English Bible, pg. 9
28. ibid
29. Proverbs 29:15

The FUTURE *is* NOW

THE FUTURE IS NOW

In the fast pace society we live in, we have no opportunity for procrastination. The future is now. Tomorrow's leaders are built today. History makers and world changers are built one day at a time.

"He will turn the hearts of the fathers to their children, and the hearts of the children to their fathers; or else I will come and strike the land with a curse." (Malachi 4:6)

The heart of God is inseparably linked with sonship and generational transfer. God's last words in the Old Testament speak of His desire for fathers and their children *(Malachi 4.6)*. God's first words in the New Testament speak of His desire toward His own Son *(Luke 3.22)*. The first words of Jesus in the New Testament speak of His desire toward His Father's house and business *(Luke 2.49)*. The first words of the devil in the New Testament are, *"If you be the Son." (Luke 4:3)*

The issues of the Kingdom of God function in the context of sonship and generational transfer. This was the case with Father, for His answer to the problem of sin was to send His Son *(John 3.16)*. It was certainly the case with Jesus as His focus while on earth was to honor His Father and complete the work Father gave Him to do *(John 17.4)*. If sonship and generational transfer was the focus of Father and Jesus, it must certainly need to be our focus as well.

THERE IS SUFFICIENT TIME

Time has been the church's greatest enemy. We have built only for today based on our assumption that Jesus could return any minute and therefore we would not have sufficient time to build right. But, history has shown us that Jesus has not returned yet, and so we would have had sufficient time to build generationally. Jesus told us it is not for us to know the times and dates pertaining to His return.[30] Our focus needs to be not *when* He will return, but *what must we obey* to hasten that return.

The time to obey is now. The time to build our sons and daughters is now. It is certain that the future will come, but what the future holds for the generations to come is predicated upon the action we take now. To build a generation is much easier than to repair it. We must seize the future now and begin to lay the building blocks of the future that guarantee a spiritual inheritance for the generations to come.

Seizing The Future

The future will be:

> > Fatherless, faithless and forceful
> > Universal, unforgiving and undivided
> > Tribal, tested and triumphal
> > Ungrateful, uprooted and unveiled
> > Religious, rebellious and redeemed
> > Entangled, entrusted and encouraging

The future promises to be many things. Generational thinkers must prepare prophetically. The complexion of life is changing rapidly. What my generation faced as youth is quite different from what our children are facing today. Temptation is not necessarily worse; it is simply different and perhaps more complex.

As we gird ourselves for action, we must understand that the future will be:

> Fatherless

"Defend the cause of the weak and fatherless..." (Psalm 82:3) God is a Father to the fatherless.[31] To carry the heart of God is to carry a father's heart for the disinherited, the disenfranchised and the discouraged.

Tragic divorce rates, unyielded hearts and a land under a curse have left a generation of fatherless children both naturally and spiritually. To reverse the curse on this land the natural and the spiritual fathers must return to their post of leadership and extend their hearts to the generations to follow.

> Faithless

The Apostle Paul speaks of the wrath of God being poured out upon a people who did not think it worthwhile to retain the knowledge of God.[32] This wrath results in, among other things, the people becoming faithless.

The generations to come will be masked with increased cynicism, anger and faithlessness. But what an opportunity for the Gospel to shine. In the

Wow. God help me not only hear but to DO.

void of faith, the church must come forth proclaiming the Gospel of the Kingdom of God. As it does, faith will be restored to those who yield their way to the Lord, for the Word of God promises, *"If we are faithless, He will remain faithful, for He cannot disown Himself." (II Timothy 2:13)*

> Forceful

Extraordinary times call for extraordinary leaders. The vacuum caused by the fatherlessness and the faithlessness of a people calls for the church to rise in forceful advance and proclaim boldly the good news of the Kingdom of God. *"... The Kingdom of Heaven has been forcefully advancing, and forceful men lay hold of it." (Matthew 11:12)* The force spoken of here is not a forcefulness of control, but a force of energy and intention. Parents must begin to live purposefully. The times in which we live are not times of peace; they are times of war. It is time to awaken the warrior spirit and lead our children into battle.

> Universal

The world today is becoming a village. Increased travel, the Internet and expansion of corporations into the global marketplace have broken down many of the walls that divided the nations. The nations are becoming one big melting pot of philosophy and practice. Travel that once took months to accomplish now is achieved in hours. Instruction that once required travel is now accomplished in cyberspace without even leaving your home.

The universalization of man means the challenging of beliefs we hold in isolation. The more our children are exposed to other faiths and cultures, the more their beliefs are challenged. If we have trained them in the belief of absolutes and how to stand up for their convictions, this can be incredibly helpful to our children's faith.

> Unforgiving

Timothy tells us the last days will be marked by terrible times. Among the terrible things that will take place is the fact that people will be unforgiving.[33] The lack of fathering and the void of faith will result in an anger and bitterness that will eat like a cancer within.

As parents, we must be there for our children to prevent them from being attacked by these terrible times. We must also become spiritual fathers and mothers to those who have become the children in the void.

> Undivided

God always has His remnant. Even in the midst of a fatherless, faithless and unforgiving generation, the Holy Spirit will raise up a people with undivided hearts and undistracted devotion. *"I will give them an undivided heart and put a new spirit in them…" (Ezekiel 11:19)*

As parents, we must model and teach our children to be undivided in their loyalty and devotion to Jesus Christ.

> Tribal

Though the future will become increasingly universal, it will at the same time become increasingly tribalistic. The future will mean the universality of experience, but the tribalism of relationship. It seems as the world opens, man's ability to relate and get along with each other closes. Loyalty has not opened with man's ability to travel.

Acceptability has not increased with technology. With the increase of pride and self-centeredness comes the increase of tribalism and nationalistic sentiment.

> Tested

Do not be misled. God will not remain silent in the midst of these terrible times. As He always has, He will be quite involved, shaking what can be shaken and testing the quality of each man's work.[34] As parents, we must pray that the quality of our parenting will be tested early on to assure we have the necessary time to rebuild if need be. Continual self-examinations along the way will keep us from irreversible setbacks with our children. We need to test and examine whether or not we have our children's hearts. We know we are losing our children's hearts when they begin to resist our authority, challenge our beliefs, withdraw communicatively, withhold affection, prefer to be with others and express cynicism.

> Triumphal

"But thanks be to God, who always leads us in triumphal procession in Christ." (II Corinthians 2:14) The key to our triumph is an abiding relationship with Jesus Christ. As long as we abide in Him through intimacy and devotion, we triumph. This does not mean the pathway will not be marked with failure and necessary adjustments. It simply means that out of personal relationship to Jesus, the Holy Spirit has our ear in which to speak and correct

our direction. As long as we remain plugged into Jesus, our victory is assured.

> Ungrateful

Another mark of the last days is that people will be disobedient to their parents and ungrateful.[35] Ungratefulness will be a sign of the future. It will be the fruit of a philosophy rooted in self-centeredness—the result of no longer acknowledging God as our source, but seeing man as our provider.

As parents, we must train our children to see God as our sole provider. *"Every good and perfect gift is from above, coming down from the Father of heavenly lights, who does not change like shifting shadows." (James 1:17)* As we train them in this reality, they develop a heart of gratitude and thankfulness.

> Uprooted

Without absolutes, a people are without roots. It is the absolutes of a society that give it roots and keep it stable. Society is consistently forsaking its absolutes and redefining its morals. As this continues to happen, it will result in the future being uprooted and the society drifting its way into meaninglessness. It will mean the instability of a people and the insecurity of a nation.

As parents, we must hold to our absolutes and not forsake them in the heat of the battle. We must impart them to our children and train them in the way of the Kingdom.

"Watch out that you do not lose what you have worked for, but that you may be rewarded fully. Anyone who runs ahead and does not continue in the teaching of Christ does not have God; whoever continues in the teaching has both the Father and the Son." (II John 8-9)

Our goal must be the full reward. To be fully rewarded we must continue in the teaching we have received from the generations before, being careful not to lose what we have worked for. Then the generations to come may also receive their benefits.

> Unveiled

"Now the Lord is the Spirit, and where the Spirit of the Lord is, there is freedom. And we, who with unveiled faces all reflect the Lord's glory, are being transformed into His likeness with ever-increasing glory, which comes from the Lord, who is the Spirit." (II Corinthians 3:17-18)

good

Transformation is the only way to lasting change. Without the Holy Spirit, the best that man can expect is symptom management. He is left to managing the fruit of his godless philosophy. But, the way of the Kingdom is the way of transformation wherein we are changed from the inside out.

The key to transformation is intimacy. We must train our children to behold the Lord. We must train them to spend time in His presence, daily looking to Jesus, the author and finisher of our faith.[36]

> Religious

The more godless man becomes, the more religious he becomes as well. By created design man must relate to something bigger than himself. If man replaces God, he will fill His absence with something to pacify the void. Pleasure, wealth, achievement, religion and others are all man's attempt to fill the void left by a godless philosophy.

The more God is reduced and redefined, the more man will create religious substitutes in an attempt to fill the vacuum, *"having a form of godliness but denying its power..." (II Timothy 3:5)* Without God, man resorts to form. He tries to appease himself with outward demonstrations that do not capture the heart. Angel worship, crystal therapy, and the rise of the occult are all examples of man's propensity toward religion.

As parents, we must be sure that we are leading our children into the full surrender of their hearts. We must learn to discern what their hearts are saying, not their words or their outward signs. Without a genuine heart response to the Kingdom of God, their experience with God will be nothing more than religion.

> Rebellious

"Do not let anyone deceive you in any way, for that day will not come until the rebellion occurs..." (II Thessalonians 2:3) The last days will be marked by increased rebellion. Already we are seeing the signs of the times. "Question authorty" is the motto of the day. Society is rapidly becoming authority neutral. Enlightenment is the philosophy of the day. We are all equal; so therefore, authority is not needed. Consequently, we make suggestions to our children rather than direct them. We bribe them to do the right thing rather than command them, as did Abraham.

Children today are left to themselves. The fruit of egalitarianism has given birth to an unprecedented level of parental frustration. The frustrations of parents have led many to abandon expectation in hopes of alleviating disappointment. Logic says, if you don't expect anything of them, you will not be disappointed. It has become common practice to hear parents tell their children to do something and then say nothing when the child answers no. The silence is indicative that the parent did not expect the child to obey.

When children grow up thinking they are equal to those in authority, they rebel without thought. A child's fear of God is formulated by their respect and honor of their parents. If children are not trained to respect and honor their parents and those in authority, they will carry no fear of God.

> Redeemed

Redemption is the gift that keeps on giving. It carries with it both the initial power to ransom us from sin and the ongoing power to buy back the freedom we have traded away.

Whatever the circumstance of our past, whatever the present condition of our children, the redemptive power of God is able to ransom our lives and buy back our freedom and the freedom of those we have lost.

Webster defines redeem, "to release through ransom; to liberate from obligation or liability; to set free by paying the price; to repurchase what has been sold."

"For the grace of God that brings salvation has appeared to all men. It teaches us to say 'No' to ungodliness and worldly passions, and to live self-controlled, upright and godly lives in this present age, while we wait for the blessed hope—the glorious appearing of our great God and Savior, Jesus Christ, who gave Himself for us to redeem us from all wickedness and to purify for Himself a people that are His very own, eager to do what is good. These, then, are the things you should teach. Encourage and rebuke with all authority. Do not let anyone despise you." (Titus 2:11-15)

Jesus Christ gave Himself to buy back this generation and the generations to come from all wickedness and to purify for Himself a people who are His very own. That includes you, me and the generations after us. We are the link to the generations to come. Redemption is the power of God capable of liberating from obligation those who may have fallen away. Redemption is the anchor of our hope. We do not hope in a vacuum. Our hope is rooted in the redemptive power of God who is capable of ransoming and repurchasing anyone who has been sold.

Yes, the future may be fatherless, faithless, unforgiving, religious, and rebellious, but in light of the redemptive power of God, we have cause to celebrate.

> Entangled

Distractions are a primary strategy of the devil. He is subtle in his workings and indirect in his attack. The enemy's intent is not to steal our children's destiny, only to entangle them so they will give their destiny away by default. His intent is not to rob us of our generational transfer, only to cause us to be so busy, we will not do what is necessary for the transfer.

The future promises to be an entangled one. The faster society becomes, the more entangled it becomes. The more technical it becomes, the more entangled it becomes. Computers promised to save us time but the very thing invented to save time is now a major consumer of it. Parents, we must learn to sort through the entanglements and focus on the eternals. We must model for our children and the generations to come a life free of all that entangles.

"Therefore, since we are surrounded by such a great cloud of witnesses, let us throw off everything that hinders and the sin that so easily entangles, and let us run with perseverance the race marked out for us." (Hebrews 12:1)

If there ever was a verse of generational transfer this is it. The writer of Hebrews spells out both our accountability to the past and our accountability to the future, and for the sake of both, he admonishes us to live an entangled free life.

> Entrusted

"...I felt I had to write and urge you to contend for the faith that was once for all entrusted to the saints." (Jude 3) All that we own and are is an entrustment. One of the most sacred entrustments we have is the stewardship of the life and faith of our children. Given to us as a trust, we must lovingly lead them into the fullness of their destiny and prepare them to do the same for the generation that will follow them. We must guard this good deposit that was entrusted to our care with the help of the Holy Spirit.[37] We must set our sights high for our children, never being satisfied that they just live

with the blessing of God, but training them to be world changers and history makers.

> Encouraged

"For I know the plans I have for you, declares the Lord, plans to prosper you and not to harm you, plans to give you a hope and a future." (Jeremiah 29:11) In this passage Father sows into our destiny by planting in our spirits the hope of a future. As parents we must plant the hope of future generations in the hearts of our children. To destroy a people, all one must do is cut them off from their future. This is first done philosophically. Years ago, the church was cut off from its future by the expectation of being raptured at any moment. Once this concept was sown into the church, it quit sacrificing for its future and stopped living from a generational mindset.

Once again the trumpet blast of generational transfer is being sounded. The Holy Spirit is coming to the church with the sound of generational accountability. It is a return to the Ancient Path. It is a willingness to be culturally irrelevant to a culture that has forsaken its root and abandoned the way of its forefathers.

These are days of tremendous encouragement. Not only is the sound being made, but the fathers have found the baton and the sons are eager to receive the transfer. Generational transfer is the devil's worst nightmare, and he is about to have a bad dream.

FOOTNOTES:

30. Acts 1:7
31. Isaiah 68:5
32. Romans 1:28
33. II Timothy 3:3
34. I Corinthians 3:13
35. II Timothy 3:2
36. Hebrews 12:2
37. II Timothy 1:14

PART *11*

Eight years ago when the Ancient Path was first published, God put a passion in me to carry on what the Lord has revealed to my Dad. That was Phase I: The Revelation. Now, out of school and entering new levels of training, God has brought me to Phase II: The Qualification and Authentication.

In Joshua I, God came to Joshua and said, "Moses my servant is dead. Now then, get ready to take my people into the Promised Land." How could Joshua so quickly take up where his spiritual father left off? How could God trust Joshua to be faithful in leading His chosen people? Joshua was prepared and qualified. His qualification came from the pattern of generational transfer. First Joshua watched Moses, then he worked alongside Moses, until finally, Joshua was prepared for Moses to step back and watch Joshua at work.

I want to serve the way Joshua did. I want to bring increase to the work of my father and want to impart that into my sons so that when the baton is passed, they are already running. I pray that as you read this book, you will share your revelation with your sons and daughters. You are leaving a legacy for your children now. How will you be remembered? If you are the son or daughter, share the truths of this book with your father. Malachi did not just speak of fathers turning their hearts to their sons, but we as sons, must turn ours as well. We cannot live in the desert any longer! It is time to enter the Promised Land by being prepared and qualified.

BY KYLE WILLIS, *April 2006*

When the Holy Spirit first spoke to me to agree in prayer with a man who had been in Heaven for 30 years, I thought it was a different spirit speaking to me. I certainly didn't believe in communicating with the dead and told this to whomever it was speaking with me. "He's dead and I don't talk to the dead."

"Yes, but his prayers aren't," was the instant response. "And I can't do what I promised him until this generation comes into agreement with what he prayed."

Instantly, I knew it was the Lord — Satan didn't want prayers answered — and the implications staggered me. My theology took a ninety degree turn and I entered another paradigm-adjusting season with God, one of many I've had over the years.

This book will mess with your paradigms!

Like a good chiropractic adjustment that twists and contorts your frame, then shoves your spinal chord through the table you're laying on, finally twisting your neck until you feel like a corkscrew — it hurts so good! I always rise from the table groaning, and then bend this way and that, telling the doctor "thanks." That's what I did when God adjusted me and it's what I found myself doing as I read The Ancient Path.

Norm Willis is dangerous to Satan and a threat to status quo Christianity. First of all, he is a thinking Christian. I know that may sound strange to you but so many Christians find themselves stuck in mediocrity because they're afraid to think outside of the box. Or perhaps it's because they have been told by other believers not to rock the boat. So the boat doesn't rock — nor does it go anywhere.

What I found so refreshing about this book is that it did rock my world and also got me moving — moving not into another faddish teaching, but farther along the path of Scripture. Out of the box thinking shouldn't be outside the boundaries of Scripture.

I've always known God is a generational God, but The Ancient Path gave me much greater understanding of this important truth. Before I finished the book, I was making plans to adjust some things in my life. I now believe I am thinking more like God thinks. That's what any good instructional book should do for us.

When God spoke to me about agreeing in prayer with a previous generation, He went on to say, "I need the synergy of the ages." That messed with my mind also — I had no idea what He was talking about. I do now. In the same way that two people working together can lift more than the sum of their individual abilities, so can two generations — that's synergy. It's not that complicated: when we connect, God multiplies power. Whether we're connecting with the person next to us, the generation behind us or the one in front, the generational God we serve cannot resist its appeal. He commands blessing! (See Psalm 133.)

Read this book with an open heart. God will speak to you. And when He does, you'll find yourself on an ancient path — a path of truth and a path of life. You will have more passion for today and hope for the future. Don't wait, learn how to synergize!

- Pastor Dutch Sheets

The Ancient Path: A Practical Guide

Whereas the first section of The Ancient Path dealt with the mandate of generational transfer, this second section deals with the plan of generational transfer. Mandates are good for they are the manner in which our heavenly Father communicates His heart to His children. Likewise, dreams are good for they are the manner in which Father communicates possibilities to His children. Vision is good, for it is the manner in which Father defines direction to His children. But mandates, dreams and visions all need a workable plan for us to walk in the reality of God's intent.

Father has an abundance of mandates, dreams and vision for His sons and daughters to walk in. But at the end of the day, the Holy Spirit translates them all into a plan for our execution. It is not enough to just believe a mandate. We must believe it, plan it and walk it out.

"For I know the plans I have for you says the Lord, plans to give you a future and a hope." (Jeremiah 29:11)

The future God has ordained for each one is tied directly to the plan He has for each one. The plan He has for us in His mandate followed by specific steps of action for us to follow.

This section is written in a desire to spell out some of the more practical side of generational joining. These suggestions are in no way an exhaustive list or even the most effective list, it is simply some of the structures that have worked well for us and we pray they will serve you as well.

As GOOD *as* OLD

"Thus says the Lord, Stand by the ways and see and ask for the ancient paths, where the good way is and walk in it; and you will find rest for your souls." (Jeremiah 6:16)

Whereas the Section I of The Ancient Path dealt with the mandate of generational transfer; Section II will deal with the plan of generational transfer. Mandates are good. Mandates are the manner in which Father communicates His heart to His children. Dreams are good, they are the manner in which Father communicates possibilities to His children. Visions are good. They are the manner in which Father communicates direction to His children. But mandates, dreams and vision all require a plan if one is to walk in the fullness of God's intent.

"For I know the plans that I have for you, declares the Lord, plans for welfare and not for calamity, to give you a future and a hope." (Jeremiah 29:11)

Father has mandates, dreams and visions for His sons and daughters, but at the end of the day He translates them all into plans. Mandates are essential for the advancing of God's agenda; dreams are a must for the comprehending of our possibilities; vision is imperative if we expect to track in the same direction of God. But, to reach the realm of accomplishment we will need to trust the Holy Spirit for a divinely authorized plan.

God's intent to give us a future and a hope is firmly rooted in His plan. His plan for our future and our hope is simply His mandate followed by specific steps of action for us to follow. His plan for our future and our hope is simply His dreams for His children, followed by His sovereign expectations. His plan for our future and our hope is essentially His vision for His sons and daughters, followed by His specific work prepared in advance for each to do. *(Ephesians 2:10)*

The success of a mandate will be determined by its plan. Having no plan is planning to fail. A divinely inspired mandate followed by a divinely orchestrated plan will result in a secure future and a definite hope.

A Mandate and A Plan

Section I of The Ancient Path defined the Kingdom mandate for generational joining and generational transfer. Section II is the specific plan to see that mandate carried out. This manual will focus on training and serve as a practical guide for generational planning. Like all plans, it will only be effective if it is followed with intentionality. Generational transfer is automatic. Whether for good or for evil, generational transfer just happens. For what you transfer to be good you must become very intentional and enter into this process with the mindset of training. Though written primarily from the perspective of the natural family, it most certainly applies to spiritual parenting as well. The intent is you would read and apply the process both to the natural children in your life and to those spiritual children entrusted to your care. Your children are destined by God to become champions. God knew them before they were formed in their mother's wombs and appointed for works prepared in advance for them to do (*Genesis 1:5; Ephesians 2:10*), He already sees them as champions. But for their champion status to be realized in time/space, they must be brought into strict training.

"Do you not know that those who run in a race all run but only one receives the prize? Run in such a way that you may win. Everyone who competes in the games exercises self control in all things... Therefore I run in such a way as not without aim..." (*I Corinthians 9:24-26*)

Children are born; champions are trained. To reach the level of the victor, you must compete so as to win. To bring our children into the fullness of their destiny and secure their generational line, parents must parent so as to raise champions.

BACK TO BEFORE

Before we can fully embrace the plan we must clearly understand the mandate. The mandate for the generations takes us all the way back to before. Back before there was time, before there was human desire, back before distractions and sin, Father defined His intention for man. An intention theologians have labeled "The Dominion Mandate."

"Then God said, 'Let us make man in Our image, according to Our likeness and let them rule over the fish of the sea and over the birds of the sky and over the cattle and over all the earth and over every creeping thing that creeps on the earth.' And God created man in His own image, in the image of God He created him, male and female He created them. And God blessed them and God said to them, 'Be fruitful and multiply and fill the earth and subdue it and over the fish of the sea and over the birds of the sky and over every living

thing that moves on the earth.'" (Genesis 1:26-28)

This four-fold commission to man is central to the works prepared in advance for us to do, that the apostle Paul refers to in Ephesians 2:10. The first and foremost arena for this commission to be realized in is the family. To parent with the mandate of dominion in mind, we must embrace this four-fold commission.

DOMINION COMMISSION STEP ONE – "BE FRUITFUL"[1]

As parents arm themselves with Father's original intention of bearing the likeness of Christ and bringing Kingdom purposes on the earth, their children will come into the fullness of their God-ordained design. Dominion of the earth is to be won one family at a time, one child at a time.

The primary thing parents are to "cause to be" is godly offspring. God is the generational Father who seeks fathers and mothers who will live their lives as bridges laid down for the generations to come. The heart of God for godly offspring is found in Malachi 2:13-15.

"Another thing you do, you flood the altar with tears. You weep and wail because He no longer pays attention to your offerings or accepts them with pleasure from your hands. You ask why, it is because the Lord is acting as a witness between you and the wife of your youth, because you have broken faith with her ... Has not the Lord made them one? In flesh and spirit they are His, and why one? It is because He was seeking godly offspring."

Malachi reveals God's heart in the marriage covenant is godly offspring. The central purpose of the marriage covenant is not the pleasure of the husband or wife, but the pleasure of God. It's the pleasure that comes when the father and mother produce godly offspring—not just offspring, but godly offspring. God did not join husband to wife so together they could produce a child then leave that child to itself and rationalize its rebellion with a "kids will be kids" justification. Kids won't be kids if parents will be parents. If parents, primarily fathers, will invest their lives into their children "causing things to be" through a lifestyle of training and character development, their children will emerge as champions and fulfill their work prepared in advance for them to do.

"Causing things to be" requires parents who will engage their parenting role with intentionality. Proverbs 29:15 says that "a child left to himself disgraces his mother." Intentionality is what this training manual is all about. The purpose of this section is to equip you conceptually and then direct you practically with specific things you can do to parent with intentionality and cause things to be in your generational line.

Dominion Mandate Step Two — "Replenish the Earth"[2]

There are two key elements in this step of the commission:

1. Intent — We already saw in Malachi 2:13-15 that God's intent was godly offspring.

2. Accomplishment — *Proverbs 22:6* tells us the pathway to accomplishment is through training. *"Train up a child in the way he should go. Even when he is old he will not depart from it."* This word for train is the Hebrew word "chanak." It means to initiate, to teach, to dedicate and to consecrate.[3] The word is only used five times in the Old Testament. Four of them have to do with the dedication of property. One was the dedication of a house and three were the dedication of the temple of Solomon. Even as Solomon dedicated the house of the Lord for the purposes of God, so too must parents dedicate and train their children for their God-given purpose.

To train a child in the way they should go is to understand there is "the Way" for the child and there is "their way" for the child. "The Way" is the universal way of the Lord that all must follow. "Their way" is that child's specific task prepared in advance for them to do that serves "the Way." Parents must discover their child's specific way and then train them in that way if they are to "confirm intent through accomplishment." The specific way for one child may be business, the way for another may be teaching, for another it may be pastoring, and for another is may be homemaking. Whatever that child's work prepared in advance for them to do is, they must be trained in that way for them to "confirm intent through acco plishment" and stay in the Way.

Accomplishment requires training. Mastery of any craft is not automatic. This is certainly true of our dominion mandate. If Mr. Woods could train Tiger from a toddler to play golf, how much more should we be training our generations in Kingdom purpose?

This section will pursue the practical steps to train the generations in pursuit of the Kingdom, spiritual intimacy, practical holiness, Kingdom culture, personal giftedness and so much more.

Dominion Commission Step Three — "Subdue the Earth"[4]

The battle for the generations is not a battle of external force. The battle for the generations is the subduing of our children's hearts. The parent's rule is not a rule of external control, but one of internal influence. It may begin with the control of children as we described in the chapter "A Will to Rule." But as they grow our children must be trained to respond to influence and remain yielded to their own self-government.

Influence is won through trust. Trust is not just a good thing. When it comes to the joining of the generations and passing truth through the generations, trust is everything. When one loses the trust of their children, they flat lose. No progress will be made in generational advance until trust is restored.

Obedience can be demanded, but trust must be won. If trust has been lost it is won back through:

1. Repentance. Put on humility and acknowledge the wrongdoing that broke the trust. Remember trust is further destroyed if one makes a practice of repentance only to commit the wrongdoing over again.

2. Centering Your Life in Christ. Trust is won by the modeling of a Christ-centered lifestyle and pursuit of the Kingdom of God. As children see their parents living for Christ and not for themselves, it lays a rock-solid foundation of trust in their lives.

3. Being Parents of their Word. Hypocrisy is the number one thief of trust. When children see their parents one way at home and another way at church, they lose trust. When they hear their parents say one thing and do another, it undermines their trust. Trust is won through integrity and being people of our word.

The paramount issue facing families today is trust between the generations. We need fathers who will protect the virtue of their children and in so doing lay the foundation of trust. We need parents who will command their children according to biblical principle and in so doing lay the foun-

key:
trust

dation of trust. We need parents who fear God enough to know when to say no and when to say yes and in so doing bring their children into subjection to God's created order of intent.

Dominion Commission Step Four – "Have Dominion"[5]

Dominion and the raising of godly offspring has to do with aligning, guarding and preserving Father's original intent for the generations entrusted to our care. We do not own our children; they belong to God and are given to us only as a stewardship. Consequently, we must steward them in complete accountability to God's expectation for child raising, not current culture.

Sustaining what was previously subdued is a tremendous responsibility. It is a responsibility for which we have been given the power of the Holy Spirit to follow, but nevertheless a responsibility. Our lack of biblical alignment to original intent has produced, in the church, a form of spiritual promiscuity.[6] Parents at large love biblical truths that produce pleasure. They will flock to teaching on prosperity, empowerment and promotion, but neglect the teachings on generational transfer, discipleship, ruling and subduing. Pleasure truths are an essential part of God's council, but alone they will not lead to dominion.

To sustain over time what was previously subdued will require parents willing to:

1. Invest Time. In a child's heart, love equals time spent. Deuteronomy 6 is the pattern for parental investment. We are commanded in verse 9 to "teach these words diligently to your sons and daughters as you sit in your home, walk by the way, when you lie down and when you get up." The pattern in the command calls for quality time and quantity time. Please understand, there is no substitution for quality time with our children, but quality in and of itself is not enough. Young children in particular don't have the sophisticated thought process to reason out quality versus quantity. All they know is my dad and mom don't seem to spend much time with me. So never forsake quality time but be sure that your family is getting enough quantity with their quality.

Some practical suggestions on investing time would be for fathers to be the ones who put their children to bed at night. Don't just send them to bed, put them to bed as Deuteronomy 6 suggests. As you do:

> Talk to them about their day, filter out negative perspectives that got on them.

identity → Speak to them about who they are. Remind them they are a son and daughter of God.

> Speak to them about your love for them, affirm them.
> Prophesy over them.
> Read the Word to them.
> Pray over them and teach them to pray with you.

In all of this you are modeling Kingdom pursuit and what it means to be a priest in the house.

Another suggestion would be weekly dates with your child. This would be uninterrupted time with just them and their dad. Perhaps it would be a breakfast, a lunch, some evening every week for an hour. It could be a Saturday morning to McDonald's for breakfast and a stop at the park on the way home.

I have had breakfast with each of my three children since the time they started school. Every Monday is with Kelsey, Tuesday is Kaleb, Wednesday is Kyle. No one or nothing takes their time. I will not schedule appointments during their time. This time is their time. We go to breakfast and just talk about where they are, and dream about the future. We pray together, go through the Word together, and just be together. In the twenty years I've been with my daughter, that is some 1,040 breakfasts together. It's some 570 with Kaleb and 780 with Kyle. We can't cover everything in these breakfast times but over the years this time adds up to communicate the depth of my love.

TO SUSTAIN OVER TIME WHAT WAS PREVIOUSLY SUBDUED WILL REQUIRE PARENTS WILLING TO:

2. WIN RESPECT. Parents win respect by being what they expect of their children. If parents expect their children to pursue a daily love relationship

with Christ, they must model that daily love relationship. If parents expect their children to obey authority, parents must model submission to the authority of their pastors and bosses. You will win the respect of your children as you model:

> Abandoned pursuit of the Kingdom of God — Your children must see you sacrificing carnal desires for your pursuit of the Kingdom.
> Covenantal love for your spouse — The greatest gift a father can give their children is to love their mother.
> Committed love for the church — It's no wonder some children don't want to go to church after hearing their parents speak so negatively of it.
> Internal integrity/External integration — Rightly related to God and rightly related to man.

The respect and trust of your family is a treasure to be fought for and sustained over time. You never fully win their respect. You win it again every day. The eye gate is a powerful thing. Let your children see you spend time with the Lord. When they wake in the morning they should never see you in bed, they should see you building an altar to God. *ex. my parents so true!*

To sustain over time what was previously subdued will require parents willing to:

3. Speak Identity. Ask God for a Kingdom vision for your wife and children, then speak what you see over them. It was Adam who named his wife and children. It was to him that Father God gave the responsibility of identification and direction. Pray for vision, then step out in boldness and speak that vision into their spirits. God chose Abraham because He knew Abraham would command his children (*Genesis 18:19*). Don't leave your child to themselves. Speak identity, speak direction, speak encouragement, speak correction. Use the evening time of putting them to bed to speak all of these things into their spirits.

As they get older, speak to them concerning their calling and the works God has prepared in advance for them to do. Remind them their life is not *Yes* their own for they were bought with a price. Don't let them settle for a career when they have received a calling. Tell them who they are, train them in who they are, invest money in who they are.

A practical suggestion would be to have each child write a paper answering these questions:

> Who am I?
> Why am I here?
> Where am I going?

[handwritten in margin: good Q's]

Update this paper at every significant milestone in their life, i.e., graduation from high school, graduations from college, marriage, children, etc.

TO SUSTAIN OVER TIME WHAT WAS PREVIOUSLY SUBDUED WILL REQUIRE PARENTS WILLING TO:

4. PROTECT THEIR CHILDREN'S DESTINY. We live in a culture that worships sex. To be those who understand the times is to be parents who protect their sons from becoming predators and their daughters from becoming targets. In this stage of the commission we clearly see that the dominion mandate must begin at home.

[handwritten in margin: personal revival before others]

TO PROTECT THE DESTINY OF OUR CHILDREN WE MUST BE PARENTS WHO ARE WILLING TO:

> Conquer and bring into submission our children's entertainment. This is not to suggest some form of legalistic ban on television and movies. It is simply to say most of the world's entertainment is saturated with sex, so we must exercise parental government and train our youth to exercise self-government in all of these expressions. This would be especially true for those who access the internet and cable television. Filters on the internet and blocks on certain channels are the very least that should be done. Music would be another key area to govern.

Conquer and bring into subjection the manner in which our children form relationships. More will be said about undistracted devotion in a later chapter. Most of us can remember the hurtful effects dating had on our hearts as we grew up. Kids would "break up" and be devastated for weeks. The mandate we have as parents is to raise our children in undistracted devotion to the Lord. (I Corinthians 7:35) We must train them in covenantal commitments without break-ups. Dating is purely a cultural experience

[handwritten in margin: → yes]

that has no foundation in biblical practice or design. To protect their destiny, we must help them not awaken love before its time. *God as #1!*

Someone has defined Father as "He who decides." As fathers we must carry the heart of God for our children and not be afraid to make decisions, even when it may be the unpopular decision. We must remember that Jesus is the Way *(John 14:6)* and we are those of the Way *(Acts 9:2)*. We must discern the cultural ways of the Jesus nation and train up our children in those ways, thereby protecting their destiny.

To sustain over time what was previously subdued will require parents willing to:

5. Satisfy the Heart. Above all else a parent must be willing to guard the children's heart, for it is the wellspring of life *(Proverbs 4:23)*. If you lose your child's heart you lose. Legalism is a heart thief. Permissiveness is a heart thief. You keep your child's heart as you are led by the Spirit in when you say "yes" and when you say "no."

win

You win the child's heart as a result of investing time, winning respect, speaking identity and protecting their destiny. All of these mixed with love, humility and prayer result in your children giving you their hearts and you giving them yours.

The purpose of this book is to help parents keep the heart of their child or winning that heart back if it has been lost. With God is it never too early or never too late to win it back. Through this book you will find practical helps and guidance to do just that. Let the Holy Spirit work deep first in you, then allow Him to guide you step by step in the winning back of your child's heart.

Being and Doing

You will find in this section a blend of the conceptual and the practical. The conceptual is written to provide context and understanding. The practical is written to provide steps of action for the joining of generations and the transfer of truth to the generations. The suggestions given are time proven suggestions. They are certainly not exhaustive, but they are effective. Follow them and they will bear fruit in your family, but above all else, follow the Holy Spirit for He is your guide.

It Is Never Too Late

In light of the redemptive power in Christ, it is never too late to start the journey of generational joining and generational transfer. You may be getting this truth late in your parenting and have already lost the heart of your child. If so, be of good courage; it is never too late to win that heart back. This section will define a clear pathway to follow for the winning or the winning back of the heart.

good practical ✶

Take a Step

1. Take inventory of your life and the life of your family.
   > Do you have the hearts of your children?
   > Is your current investment enough to bring them into the fullness of their destiny?
   > Pray for the turning of your heart to your children and your chidren's heart to you. *(Malachi 4:6)*

2. Do you have a Kingdom vision for your children?
   > Do you see them after the Spirit?
   > Pray now for a Kingdom vision for each child.

3. Do you have a training strategy that will equip your children to fulfill the work prepared in advance for them to do?
   > Do you have a sense of their calling?
   > Have you discerned their giftings?
   > Are you pursuing a plan to develop and advance in seed form?

4. What do you admire most in the fathers and mothers you respect?
   > Write out a list of the admired qualities.

5. What must change in you for the admired qualities to be practiced by you?
   > Write out a strategy for that desired change.

> Share that strategy with the one you are accountable to.

> Ask your accountability to keep you accountable to your plan.

Recommended Reading Along the Path

1. *The Ancient Path* by Pastor Norm Willis, Christ Church Publishing.

2. *You Have Not Many Fathers: Recovering the Generational Blessing* by Mark Hanby, Destiny Image Publishers.

3. *Raising a Modern Day Knight: A Father's Role in Guiding His Son to Authentic Manhood* by Robert Lewis, Focus on the Family Publishers.

Each chapter will include a recommended reading list appropriate for that specific stage of the journey. To maximize the effect of each stage, it is recommended you read as many of the suggested books as possible. This will give opportunity for the Holy Spirit to deepen the revelation and define specific steps of action.

Footnotes

1. "Be fruitful" literally means to "cause things to be." Strong's Concordance #6509

2. "Replenish the earth" literally means to "confirm intent through accomplishment." Strong's Concordance #4390

3. Lyrical Aids to the Old Testament, Key Word Study Bible, #2396.

4. "Subdue the earth" literally means to "conquer and bring into subjection anything contrary to God's created order." Strong's Concordance #3533

5. "Have dominion" literally means to "sustain over time what was previously subdued." Strong's Concordance #7278

6. Promiscuity is defined as "the enjoyment of pleasure without the acceptance of responsibility."

A Generation of His Presence

"Come, let us return to the Lord.
He has torn us to pieces
but He will heal us;
He has injured us
but He will bind up our wounds.
After two days He will revive us;
on the third day he will restore us,
that we may live in His presence.
Let us acknowledge the Lord;
let us press on to acknowledge Him.
As surely as the sun rises,
He will appear;
He will come to us like the winter rains
like the rains that water the earth."
(Hosea 6:1-3)

In a fallen world where mankind is prone to sin, the presence of God is everything. In a world where Christ-likeness is our goal, it is imperative that we learn how to live in the presence of God and train those we lead to do the same. Hope is one of the distinguishing factors that separate us as believers from the rest. The foundation of that hope is the Holy Spirit and the presence of God He brings.

Though God is omnipresent, meaning His presence is everywhere, there is still the need to come into the tangible or manifest presence of God on a daily basis. Jesus knew of sweet communion with the Father moment by moment. But He still made it His practice to set aside the early hours to come before His Father and offer that time up as the first fruits of His day. Learning to spend time in the Lord's presence and training those we lead to do the same is the most fundamental thing we will ever do and the most profound. It's fundamental in that it must be primary, yet it is profound in that it doesn't come naturally. Becoming a people of His presence is a process that requires training and discipline. You would think something as awesome as the presence of God would not require training to enjoy, but due to the warfare resisting it and the flesh that must be crossed to practice it, becoming a people of His presence requires training.

Trained to Come Before the Lord

In the Old Testament times a whole process was to take place before the priest could come before the Lord. Because of the veil that hung between the Holy of Holies and the Holy Place, man was separated from God's presence. Only one man, the high priest, was permitted to go beyond the veil into the presence of God and he was only permitted to do so once a year, or the Day of Atonement (*Leviticus 16:1-19*). To go in he was to take the blood of the bull and the goat for his sins. So to come before the Lord certain designated times required offerings, specific clothing and bathing ceremonies had to be observed lest the priest die. But I'm afraid in light of the New Testament grace we "show up" with very little preparation or heart training. Please understand what I am saying. When the veil was torn in two at the crucifixion, we were granted free access into God's presence by the shed blood of Christ and His shed blood alone. Though the blood grants us free access, it doesn't free us from the need of certain preparations and processes. This training to come before the Lord is not what gives us the access, the training is what enables us to appropriate what the free access affords. Coming before the Lord is a lifelong process that begins with training ourselves and our children in particular to:

[handwritten margin notes: wow! break familiarity]

1. Posture the Heart – Proverbs 4:23

"Above all else guard the heart for it is the wellspring of life." Offering up to the Lord the first fruits of our day must never be seen as on obligation or some form of religious duty. Coming before the Lord is life's ultimate privilege. So our hearts must be postured in privilege rather than obligation for us to interact with the Lord as He intends.

Our children in particular must be trained in the privilege of waiting on God. From an early age they must be trained to see the delight of seeking God, not just the discipline. This training comes by way of parental example. As they see the parents delighting to offer up to God the first fruits of the day, they will be inclined to do the same. To learn by example, your children must see their parents spending time with the Lord. They must hear of their pursuit of God and they must see the fruits of that pursuit. If every morning when the children rise, they see their parents in bed, they

[handwritten margin notes: yes help me to listen]

will learn that sleep is the virtue of value. Whereas, upon waking they see their parents before the Lord in prayer and reading of the Word, they will learn that devotion is the virtue of value.

Many fathers in particular say, "I pray in the car on the way to work and read my Bible during my breaks." That is well and good, but it carries no impact for generational transfer. For your devotional life to have a generational impact your children must see, hear and experience your pursuit of God.

A heart postured correctly is one that keeps our devotional pursuit from becoming familiar or legalistic. Both extremes will rob us of God's presence and circumvent our generational transfer in this regard.

"Blessed are those who have set their heart on pilgrimage." (Psalm 84:5) The correct heart posture is one that sees our pursuit of God as that of a lifelong pilgrimage, wherein we are in pursuit of life's ultimate privilege and training those we lead in its pursuit as well.

2. SET THE MIND – COLOSSIANS 3:1-2

"If then you have been raised up with Christ, keep seeking the things above where Christ is seated at the right hand of God. Set your mind on the things above not on the things of the earth." Psalm 84:5

Because the Christian life is an exchanged life, we must develop a mindset of the daily exchange wherein we present our inabilities in exchange of His sufficiency. This exchange can never be seen as a one time event or a situational event. The exchange of His life for ours must be seen as a daily process. Our children must be trained not to trust in soul strength or self life. They must be taught to present themselves upon the altar morning by morning to receive a fresh supply of Christ's life. It's in this reality they discover coming before the Lord is not a religious obligation we fulfill out of duty; it is a matter of spiritual life and death that we fulfill out of deepest joy and desperation. This mindset does not always come naturally, especially in the beginning of their process when they don't perceive much benefit coming from the process. It is at this stage they must be taught two vital principles:

A. SEEKING GOD FOR NAUGHT – We must be content to seek the Lord

Yes!

because He is worthy to be sought, not because we will always receive something. Revelation, illumination, direction, provision, etc., are all good reasons to seek the Lord, but He should be sought even if those benefits are not perceived. Our children must be trained to seek the face of the Lord, not just His hand of provision. Having said that, our Father is a Father who provides abundantly and lavishes His love upon His children, but we seek Him primarily for who He is, not what He gives.

B. PERCEIVED BENEFIT VS. SPIRITUAL BENEFIT — Whether one perceives benefit coming from their pursuit of God or not, they are still benefiting. Jesus said, *"The words I speak to you, they are spirit and they are life." (John 6:63)* Though the mind may not perceive immediate benefit, the spirit is receiving life. So whether or not the mind is informed, the spirit is being edified.

Jesus also said, "You are cleansed through the word spoken to you." *power of Word of God* There is a spiritual cleansing taking place each time we read the Word whether we perceive ourselves being cleansed or not. Though we are developing a mindset to seek the Lord, our mind is not the primary faculty we are seeking to develop. We certainly do want to educate our minds, but the spirit is our first faculty of development that we seek to build.

Another key benefit that transpires whether perceived or not is blessing. Revelation 1:3 reads *"Blessed is he who reads and those who hear the words of the prophecy and heed the things that are written."* John promises a blessing to the reader and hearer of God's words. Whether perceived or not, the reader and hearer are being blessed.

Our children must be trained to seek God for who He is and then know deep in their knower that they are benefiting even when they may not perceive they are.

3. INCLINE THE EAR — PSALM 45:10

"Listen, O daughter, give attention and incline your ear." (John 15:3) To incline your ear is to listen with intention. It is to become very purposeful in your listening. Jesus spoke of the possibility of having ears to hear but not hearing *(Matthew 11:15)*. An inclined ear is the opposite of this condition. An inclined ear is first a heart condition. An inclined ear is an unfamiliar ear. An inclined ear is a yielded ear. An inclined ear is an ear willing to hear

and willing to obey what is heard.

Our children must be trained to listen to God. It is never enough to just go through the motions of coming before the Lord, but never hearing Him speak. Having come into the Lord's presence, our children must be trained to wait, to listen, to hear and to obey. Like getting to know any voice, it comes with time. The more you listen, the more you are able to distinguish. If someone calls you on the phone one time, they may have to identify themselves. But if they were to call daily, you would quickly reach a level of relationship where voice identification was automatic. Such is the case with hearing God's voice. It sounds a bit intimidating at first, "listening to God," but the more our children are trained to give themselves to the process, the more real it becomes.

What is heard must always be checked against the written Word and the appropriate authorities in their lives for accuracy.

4. YIELD THE WILL — LUKE 22:42

"Father, if thou art willing, remove this cup from me. Yet not my will, but thine be done." Having done all to posture the heart, set the mind and incline the ear, now the will must be surrendered so the process can do its work. Our children must be trained by our example of surrender. They must see us model a life laid down and a life surrendered to the will of God. They must be trained to see life as a seamless garment, i.e., every time their sibling crosses their will, it is training to yield their will to God. The greatest thing a parent could ever impart to their children is a hunger for the presence of God. The greatest training they could ever give is to train their children to wait, listen, hear and obey the Lord. Consequently, parents must get very intentional to never leave their children to themselves in hope of them getting it all. If the children are trained, they will respond, but it will require parents finding the ancient path and leading them in the way.

PERSONAL TRAINING AND CORPORATE PRESENCE

Let's turn our focus now to preparing ourselves and our children for the corporate presence of God. To simply attend a religious gathering requires no preparation at all, but as we saw earlier, to come into the presence of the Lord requires certain preparation. Parents in pursuit of the ancient path must never simply take their children to church. Parents in pursuit of generational transfer must train their children how to come before the Lord and be in the presence of God. The Apostle Paul understood this truth when writing to his son Timothy: *"I am writing these things to you hoping to come to you before long, but in case I am delayed I write so that you may know how one ought to conduct themselves in the household of God which is the church of the living God, the pillar and support of the truth." (I Timothy 3:14-15)*

Knowing how to conduct oneself in the house of the Lord is certainly more than not running in the halls or smoking in the restrooms. Proper conduct in the house of the Lord has more to do with preparing one's heart to come in and posturing one's mindset to go out. Conducting oneself properly in the house of the Lord is all about how we engage the corporate dynamic that takes place each time the church meets.

Proper conduct in the house of the Lord begins long before you arrive at the church building. Parents must know how to prepare themselves and then how to prepare the generations who follow, how to come in before the Lord and how to go out after the Lord has manifested His presence. We are all glad that people don't just roll out of bed on Sunday morning and come to the worship service without changing out of their pajamas, brushing their teeth and washing their hair. We are all grateful that before people come they make necessary preparations. And such should be the case spiritually. Before we arrive for any worship service, we should first prepare to come before the presence of the Lord by:

I.   Preparing our hearts
2.   Setting our minds
3.   Inclining our ears
4.   Yielding our wills

To come into His Presence

SOME PRACTICAL HELP

The preaching of the Word is like the sowing of seed (Matthew 13). For seed to take root the seed must be cultivated and tilled. The preparation of the soul often determines the yield of the crop. Following is a very practical process that we must embrace as parents and then train our children to do the same every time they come before the Lord.

1. PREPARE THE HEART – In the parable of the sower, (*Matthew 13*) Jesus likened the heart to soil. For the seed of God's Word to take root, the heart must be prepared. If the heart is hard and full of offense it will be unable to receive the seed sown. So rather than just coming before the Lord with no preparation and going out with no real interaction, we must train those we lead to come prepared.

WE PREPARE THE HEART BY:

A. BEING PRAYED UP BEFORE WE COME – This would be prayer specific to the particular meeting we are preparing our hearts for. In this time of prayer we are asking the Holy Spirit to give us the spirit of wisdom and revelation. We are asking for ears to hear and a will to do. We are asking that we would be sensitive to be used in any way the Holy Spirit would desire.

B. BEING FREE OF OFFENSE – An offended heart is a hard heart, unable to receive the engrafted word. Before we come before the Lord we must forgive any offense we might have against someone and make that relationship right.

key for unity

"If therefore you are presenting your offering at the altar and there remember that your brother has something against you, leave your offering there before the altar and go your way. First be reconciled to your brother and then come and present your offering." (Matthew 5:23-24)

Childhood is a tremendous age to be trained in the art of conflict resolution. If parents can train their children from an early age to keep the heart free of conflict and bitter root judgments, their generational transfer will transpire virtually unhindered.

C. COMING WITH EXPECTATION AND ANTICIPATION – So often it seems we get what we expect. If we expect little from the worship service, we receive little, whereas if we expect much we get much. If God is able to do exceedingly abundantly more than we could ever imagine or think (*Ephesians 3:20*) then we need to align our expectations with God's ability and desire.

All too often we train our children inadvertently to expect nothing from

God. We do so when, from an early age, we allow them to bring coloring books and other activities to keep them occupied during the worship service. So when the adults are worshipping, the children are coloring and when the message is being preached, they are reading Dr. Seuss. Though not intentionally, yet nevertheless assuredly, this trains them that worship and the word is irrelevant to them, so they need not pay attention until they are "older." The problem is, by the time they are "older," they have already judged church to be irrelevant to their life and most definitely for old people.

In the past our option has been to have "children's church" and gear the service for them so they find it relevant and come full of expectation. Though this option is viable, it does not recognize the need to join the generations and provide a platform for the fathers to train the children to worship and listen to the preaching so as to hear from God. This is not to say "children's church" is wrong; it is simply to say it is limited and should not be the every week reality for our children. Rather, the fathers and mothers should use the worship service as the context to train their children to close their eyes in worship and focus on the Lord. In this context, they need to train them to lift their hands and express their love. When the Word is being preached, they need to train them to listen. Listening begins very basically. Train them to mark down the title of the message, the primary text and all ensuing Scripture references. Ask them to mark down every time the speaker says Jesus, God, love, etc. The initial stage is training them to listen. They may not go home walking in the fullness of revelation, but they are being trained to do so.

D. BEING HUNGRY TO LEARN — *"Blessed are those who hunger and thirst for righteousness for they shall be satisfied." (Matthew 5:6)* Spiritual hunger is a virtue to be sought. If at any time spiritual hunger subsides, it must be recultivated.

The lack of hunger is generally due to the lack of application of what has already been received. Hearing the Word will only dissipate one's hunger. Those who hear the Word, apply the Word and give that Word away to others come hungry for more and as a result are blessed and satisfied.

A hungry people, full of expectation, will make an average speaker great. Conversely, a people who lack spiritual hunger will make a great speaker average. Hunger draws life out of the one speaking. The hunger and response of the people is like a catalyst that sparks the life of God in the one speaking and releases the fullness of what the Holy Spirit intends for that meeting.

Parents can help their children in this stage by processing with them for application what the child heard in that particular sermon. A parent can sit with the child, review their notes, ask them what they heard and seek for ways to make application. In so doing, the Word is being digested in the child's life and room is being made for more.

COMING BEFORE THE LORD REQUIRES A HEART PREPARATION.

2. ENGAGE IN WORSHIP — Worship is an end in itself. If all we did on a given morning is worship the Lord, we would have fulfilled our reason for coming. Having said that, worship is also a means by which we prepare the soil of our hearts to receive the Word. To engage worship is to come before the Lord with a whole heart. To not engage worship is to display a blatant disregard and familiarity with God.

Our worship should not be predicated upon how we feel, how well we like the song being sung, whether the worship leader is anointed, etc. Our worship should be predicated upon God's worth and our need to engage. If you are having difficulty engaging, here are a few suggestions:

> Sit as close to the front as possible. This eliminates distractions and places you where there seems to be a more concentrated sense of His presence. We know intellectually the presence of God in the back of the room is the same as the presence of God in the front of the room, but when it comes to engaging, the issue is not the intellectual reality, it is the tangible reality. Tangibly speaking, the presence of God seems to be more concentrated in the front of the sanctuary. Get your children in the middle of the tangible presence.

> Close your eyes and focus. You don't have to close your eyes to worship, but when you are struggling with engaging, focus is everything.

> Raise your hands, dance, and engage whatever form the worship song

expresses. The key is engagement, then feeling. Most often we say, "If I feel it, then I will engage it," but the spiritual principle is engage it, then you will feel it. So our primary reason for raising our hands, kneeling, bowing, etc., is not because we feel that way, it is because these are commanded forms of worship that must be engaged. Parents must train their children to engage worship. They must guard from getting so lost in their own expression that they fail to see their children are not expressing themselves. So in the early childhood steps in particular, they need to have one eye on God and one eye on the children to help them keep their eyes on God.

3. ENGAGE THE WORD — To engage the word is to come to church with a Bible and notebook. The foundation of generational transfer is the transfer of truth from one generation to the next. You certainly can't transfer truth you can't remember. To listen to a sermon without a Bible and notebook is a predetermined decision not to remember what was heard. The Bible instructs us to be doers of the Word, not hearers only *(James 1:22)*. You can't be a doer of something you can't remember. Coming with a Bible and notebook and writing down the key things said helps you in the ability to retain and enables you to recall the Word as well.

I suggest everyone take two sets of notes. The first is what the speaker is saying; the second is what the Holy Spirit is saying in what the speaker says.

Training our children to take notes keeps them active and engaged while in a worship service. We have sold our children short thinking they could never stay focused for an hour or two. Well they can't if they are never trained, but if they are trained they certainly are able.

4. IMPLEMENT THE WORD — Human nature is to walk away from the mirror and forget what you just saw. To remember what just transpired in worship and the Word, we must become very purposeful and intentional. To implement the Word one must be able to recall what was previously said. For the purpose of recall, notes must be organized in a way they can be referred to. I suggest you give every message you hear a title. The first page of your notebook and your child's notebook should be the table of contents. Write down the title of the message and give that message the number one. The next message will be number two. On the top right corner of the note page, write down the corresponding number with the title.

Then for recall, all you must do is look at your table of contents, see the message title and corresponding page number and then turn to those pages. However many pages you have for message one are numbered "1." However many pages you have for message two are numbered "2," and so on.

5. REVIEW THE WORD — Having organized your notes for recall, now you have the ability to review what was previously said. Review is what gives you ownership of the Word heard. Without review and personal owner-ship, it is someone else's revelation. Only when it is reviewed before the Holy Spirit and He makes the personal applications in our lives, does it really become ours.

The goal is not to fill up notebooks with notes that are never referred to. The goal is organization for recall in order to facilitate person-al application.

This is a good exercise for fathers in their weekly times of discipling their children. As you meet, go over their notes. Help them both in the content they wrote down and in the manner in which they intend to implement them.

6. PREPARE FOR THE NEXT ENCOUNTER — The process just described is a repetitive cycle. We are forever meditating on the last encounter with God and preparing our hearts for the next.

The success of our transfer from one generation to the next will largely be predicated upon how we come before the Lord and train those who fol-low us to do the same. As we train them to prepare their hearts, engage worship, engage the Word, implement the Word, review the Word and pre-pare for the next encounter, we can expect a fruitful transfer that increases with effectiveness and Christ-likeness.

TAKE A STEP

1. Parents must lead by example. If you don't already set aside the first fruits of your day, set aside a minimum of:

> 30 minutes a day in prayer.
> 30 minutes a day in Bible reading.

2. Train your children in the discipline of coming before the Lord and set-

ting aside the first fruits of their day. Start small and work up. Wake them in the morning with enough time for:

> Ten minutes in prayer. Guide them in what to pray for. Use the Lord's prayer as a format:

> Start with hallowing God: "Our Father who art in heaven,"
> Pray for Kingdom purpose: "Thy Kingdom come, Thy will be done."
> Pray for daily provision: "Give us this day our daily bread."
> Pray for relational clarity: "Forgive us our trespasses as we forgive those who trespass against us."
> Pray for spiritual protection: "Lead us not into temptation, but deliver us from evil."
> Close in praise: "For thine is the Kingdom and the power and the glory forever and ever."

> Ten minutes in Bible reading. Use a one or two year study through the Bible, or one Psalm, one Proverbs, and selected reading.

Recommended Reading Along the Path

1. *Waiting on God* by Andrew Murray, Whitaker House.
2. *Possessing Your Inheritance* by Chuck Pierce & Rebecca Wagner Systema, Renew Publishing.
3. *Don't Waste Your Life* by John Piper. Crossways Books.

Family Planning

"For I know the plans I have for you says the Lord, plans to give you a future and a hope." (*Jeremiah 29:11*)

Family planning, from a spiritual perspective, is a matter of discernment not initiation. Proper family planning is not dreaming up something by yourself, but rather discerning the plan God has already devised.

From eternity past, God has determined a plan for you and your family. That plan is one of the primary reasons you were apprehended and your family was formed. According to Ephesians 2:10, we are all "God's workmanship, created in Christ Jesus for good works which God prepared beforehand that we should walk in them."

In advance of every human plan, God had a plan. Before every independent pursuit, God ordained a plan for you to pursue. Family planning is simply discerning the works prepared in advance for us to do. To stand at the cross road and ask for the ancient path (*Jeremiah 6:16*) is to discern amidst the multitude of possibilities, the plan for your family that God prepared beforehand.

As prophet, priest and king in his family, it is the father's (or single mother's) primary responsibility to lead his family into the discovery of eternal purpose. As a priest, he is to lead his family into the presence of God where this discovery is made. As a prophet, he is to speak vision, direction and encouragement to his family along the way. As a king, he is to establish the Kingdom in his home and train his family in godly authority.

Writing a Family Mission Statement

Once a family's eternal purpose is discovered, it is wise to write that plan down in the form of a mission statement. A family mission statement simply describes (at that particular season) the vision God has given you as a family and how you plan to get there. This family mission statement should address:

> The specific plan for that particular family
> How that plan is to be accomplished

Although many families share the same priorities, a mission statement should recognize the uniqueness of each family and the individuals that represent that family. The development of this mission statement should recognize the uniqueness of each family and the individuals that represent that family. The development of this mission statement should reflect the unique personalities, giftings God has sovereignly ordained. The promise is when we train our children up in the way they should go, when they are old they will not depart. *(Proverbs 22:6)* The writing of a family mission statement is simply the discerning and recording of that preordained way which gives the family a clear focus to rally around. The mission statement becomes the family compass by which we are able to discern future direction and avoid possible distractions or detours.

"Where there is no vision, the people are unrestrained." (Proverbs 29:18)

Where there is no vision for the family, the children wander aimlessly. Without a clear sense of family purpose, children will dwell carelessly. It is the eternal focus that God ordained for the family that keeps ones heart engaged in a purpose greater than oneself. Children wander because they were never given a cause worthy of their passion. It is the call of the impossible that captures the heart and passions of the generations to come. The motto of the Kingdom family must be, "It is impossible but not too difficult." This tension of "impossibility," but "surely we can do it" is what captures the heart of the generations to come. The family mission should call the generations to the impossible then introduce them to a lifestyle of Holy Spirit dependency where they discover their means of accomplishment.

The generations are lost to the purposes of God because of boredom. We are telling them the stories of David and Goliath rather than training them to take on their own Goliath. Youth are pacifying themselves with video games where they slay demons, when they could be equipped to cast out real demons. The greatest adventure known to man is the adventure of the Spirit led walk. Our families must be infused with a passion to believe God and then be sent with an eye to represent Him.

SOUGHT AFTER: RAISING GENERATIONS OF INTENT

The purpose of this section is to enable its readers to move from possibility into possession. To move from the possibility of what could be, into the possession of what God has declared to be, requires strategic intent.

Having recently watched the 2006 Winter Olympics, I was once again reminded of the training and regiment necessary to win the gold. From the earliest of age, parents will rouse their children in the early hours of the morning so they can practice and train. Why? Because that is the price one must pay if they intend to win gold. A person's level of training will determine their level of play. Parents and children of Olympic potential are willing to pay the price because they see themselves as contenders. They are not dreamers, but parents and children of intention. They are sought after to represent the Olympic team because they are individuals of purpose, committed to a cause.

Like these champions of sport, you and I are sought after as well. We are parents of intent because there is something of critical importance that Almighty God seeks. "Has not the Lord made them one. In flesh and spirit they are His. Any why one? Because He was seeking godly offspring. (Malachi 2:15 NIV)

It strikes me as odd that God would seek after anything. I understand God declaring something to be so. I even understand God making a sovereign decree. But the notion that God would seek something and not have it is peculiar to me. My capacity would say, "God is God, and God gets what He wants." This of course is true except when it comes to the participation of man. Ultimately, God does get what He wants. The only question is, does He get it in you and me? Will He get in us the godly offspring He seeks?

In Malachi 2, the prophet tells us one thing God sought, one thing God focused His desired affection upon – that one thing was generations of godly offspring.

RULERS WITH DIVINE CONNECTIONS

According to *Strong's Concordance*, the Hebrew word for godly means, "Rulers with divine connections."[7] It speaks of a man or woman "in a position like god."[8] This not "god" in the sense of nature; it is like a god in the sense of influence. What God seeks in the purpose of marriage is a generational joining, leading to a faith transfer, resulting in a multitude of godly offspring who rise up as rulers and are released into positions of transforming influence because of their divine connections. This is the ultimate empowerment. This is the ultimate empowerment that comes because generations have been joined and divine connections have been made.

Raising generations of intent is all about being possessed with a vision larger than oneself. It is about seeing beyond the immediate, so that God might get what He seeks after. The story is told of a man walking through a rock quarry who sees three men chiseling stone. Coming up to the men he asked the first, "What are you doing?" The first man answered, "I am cutting stone." Asking the second man the same question, the second man answered, "I am working to support my family." Coming up to the third man the question was asked again. The third man answered, "I am building a cathedral." The first man saw only a job. The second man saw only provision, but the third man saw destiny. The third man saw not only what was, but he saw what would be. In each swing of the hammer he saw the cathedral locked up in that stone. Knowing it would be hundreds of years before the cathedral would be complete, he still chisled and cut while understanding the importance of each step.

Solomon understood generational vision. Though he didn't do a very good job passing it on, he did a good job receiving. In I Kings 8:20, when the Ark of the Covenant was brought back to the temple, it says, *"Solomon thanked God for permitting him to succeed his father."* Success in Solomon's mind was being generationally joined. In contrast His brother Absalom saw things different. II Samuel 18:18 reads, *"Absalom had no sons so he built a monument to himself."* Having no vision beyond himself, he built a monument. Solomon had a vision for generational joining so he built a bridge. It was a bridge of succession and inheritance. It was a bridge of legacy that joined generations past with generations yet to come.

The godly offspring that God seeks requires specific intentionality in parents. It requires a willingness to lead, a willingness to impart heart and a willingness to invest vast, copius amounts of time. There is no quick fix when it comes to raising those who will be thrust into positions of ruling and judging with divine connections.

There is nothing automatic about a positive generational transfer. Children left to themselves will disgrace their parents. That is, they will remove grace from the parenting process. What was meant to be one of life's greatest joys will become hell on earth. Why? Because children left to themselves bring the parents, the family, and the land under a curse. (*Malachi 4:6*) Without the turning of our hearts as parents to our children and, our children to us as parents, we come under the curse of God. Consequently, generations who are supposed to be joined, become generations who are cursed.

So the issue becomes, how do we reverse the curse? How do we win our children back if they are lost to the purposes of God? Let me answer that first by saying to those with younger children, it is much easier to build children than it is to repair adults, so pay the price now. You will pay the price one way or another, but it is far less painful to build than it is to rebuild.

If the generations have been lost, a family mission statement is of little use. So before we share how to write about the family's mission, let me share how to win children back who have been lost to the purposes of God and lost to the heart of the family. If you have lost your child's heart there are not quick fixes, but you can win them back. You are the parents. God has given you the keys of the Kingdom; you have authority. You are the ruler with divine connections, but for the influence of those connections to be released, there are a few things you must do.

1. You must repent.

Without repentance, Malachi says, you are under a curse. This is not about coming under condemnation or judgment; it is about getting free. Your freedom and the return of your children begins with the acknowledgment of a withheld heart. Ask the Lord to forgive you. Ask your children to forgive you for leaving them to themselves, for not prioritizing them as you should, or, for not investing in them as you would have liked to. Ask them to forgive you for not giving your heart as the Lord instructed you to. Ask them to forgive you for being hypocritical, legalistic, permissive or whatever would define as your circumstance.

2. You must pray.

No, this is not the prayer of petition in hope of something happening. This is authoritative, positional prayer where from your position of being seated with Christ in the heavenly places, you command the will of God to be done on earth just as it is in heaven. There are no estranged families in heaven; there will be no estrangement here on earth. There are no children running from God in heaven; there will be no running from God on *amen!* Earth. You are the ruler with authority and you have divine connections especially in relationship to your children, so decree their return. Decree the turning of their hearts back to God and back to you. Bind the enemies influence in their lives. There is increased power when two or three join in agreement. So gather with other family members or friends and pray for the return of the prodigals.

3. YOU MUST INVEST.

Don't relate to your children on the level of do's and don'ts. Relate to them *God* on the level of the heart. You will certainly have to speak to them about right and wrong, but do so only after investing time and heart back into the relationship. As previously stated, love means time spent. God builds relationally and connects relationally. So be like Him. Get some relational currency in your account before you make a correctional withdrawal.

Your hope for the generations is in the reality that they are sought after. Almighty God seeks their return and their joining. Don't throw away your confidence, it will be richly rewarded if you do not lose hope. You have the keys to your children's future – turn them.

BUILDING CHILDREN

While there is hope in rebuilding adults, it is far easier to build children. Building children begins from the womb and even before that. It starts with the presuppositions we carry concerning the parents responsibility to lead their children and even command them, as God had said to Abraham. (*Genesis 18:19*) The key to this responsibility of leadership is the writing of a family mission statement. Simply put, a family mission statement delineates the goals we have as a family and the way in which we plan to get there. A family mission statement answers three primary questions:

1. Who God has defined your family to be?
2. What He has determined your family to do?
3. How He expects your family to do it.

Each family mission statement should reflect the individual calling, giftings and personalities of that particular family. The goal of the statement should not be original, but truthful. It should be truthful to the who, the what and the how God has ordained for that family.

BIBLICAL EXAMPLES

The Bible gives us glimpses of mission statements written by God and by individuals to chart their course. God wrote a mission statement for Abraham's family in Genesis 18:19. Joshua wrote a mission statement for his family in Joshua 24:5. David recorded a mission statement for Solomon in I Kings 2:1-4. Though without a "nuclear" family, Paul wrote a mission statement for his life in Philippians 3:7-14. Listed below are some contemporary examples of a family mission statement.

We are a family of sons and daughters of Jesus Christ, demonstrating a Kingdom culture by training the generations to carry the vision of Christ centeredness and covenantal living through a heart of submission, with faith, passion, love and obedience, for the glory of God and the reformation of the church.

"The mission of our family is to create a nurturing place of faith, order, truth, love, happiness and relaxation and to provide opportunity for each individual to become responsibly independent and effectively interdependent in order to serve worthy purposes in society through understanding and living the gospel of Jesus Christ."

A family mission statement should be timeless, yet relevant. It should define both the direction and the means. Every member of the family should participate in a council so there is total ownership of the family plan. Like the putting together of a puzzle, each family member will bring a piece of the overall look. When the whole family contributes, it is much easier to detect what God has ordained from the foundation of time. (*Ephesians 2:10*) A family mission statement is something specially uncovered by the entire family. Therefore, it can be owned by the entire family. With family ownership ,it will serve as a roadmap to guide a means to refocus in the midst of life's storms. A family mission statement cannot simply be presented and then expected to be enthusiastically embraced. Fathers must lead the family into a council of participation and mutual discovery.

HINTS FOR THE PROCESS

Before writing your mission statement, set aside a season of prayer and even of fasting. After the predetermined prayer is done, meet to initiate the process. The first action of importance would be to identify callings, gift-ings, burdens and characteristics unique to your respective family. These callings, giftings, burdens and characteristics serve as the components that make up the context of your statement. To help this process ask yourselves:

1. What has been said prophetically over your family?
2. What are the unique passions your family holds?
3. When people look at your family, what do they see?
4. What are the core values your family holds most dear?

With all those building blocks defined, you can begin the process of dis-tilling the components to a concise three to four sentence statement that defines the who, what and how. The central focus of your mission state-ment is the eternal purpose of God. The family exists for Him first, not Him for the family.

Once you come up with a written statement, stand back from it and evaluate:

1. Is it Christ centered?
2. Does it ring true with who you are?
3. Could you pattern your life after it?
4. If followed, will this statement advance the Kingdom of God?

Once your mission statement has been distilled, tweaked and accepted, write it out for all to have and to memorize. The next step will be to dis-cuss each family member's piece in seeing the mission fulfilled.

THE PITFALLS OF GENERATIONAL TRANSFER

So far in our discussion we have only talked about the positive aspects of generational transfer. This is not to say that there are negative aspects, only to point out certain concerns that result in the transfer if we are not aware and deal with them up front. Just as the fruit of generational transfer grows more effective with each generation, so does the insidiousness of warfare. The focus of the first generation's temptation generally seems to be the obvious sins like immorality or drugs, but as the subsequent generations are apprehended, the nature of their temptation seems to get far more subtle and insidious. Instead of dealings with the outward sins of action, they deal with the inward sins of attitude. Sin becomes far more sophisticated as it shifts from outward actions to inward mindsets. It is here where parents and spiritual leaders must trust the Holy Spirit for discernment to deal with the root of the issues that face the generation, not just the fruit.

Root issues of concern

1. Entitlement - The root mindset behind entitlement is the valuing of generational inheritance above a personal discovery that would produce ownership. Spiritual inheritance is a magnificent thing, but not if it robs the generations of discovery and ownership. The most powerful inheritance we can impart to the generations to come is a heart of a seeker who is never satisfied with receiving but not owning or accepting without discovering.

The entitlement I speak of is not the entitlement of "you owe me," That would be far too obvious. This is the entitlement of, "I know I will receive." It is not a greed based entitlement; it is a an assumption based entitlement that if left unchecked, it will produce an inactive expectation.

Entitlement was the sin of Jacob. Jacob was the third in the generational line and apparently his entitlement ran so deep that he thought nothing of the fact that he was willing to lie and connive his way into an inheritance that wasn't rightly his. In both Esau and Jacob we see a willingness train below their level of gifting. Entitlement will produce a mindset that trusts more in one's gift than it does in their training. An overdeveloped gift mixed with an underdeveloped training will produce a character deficiency that will lead to disqualification. What someone with entitlement is able to build with their giftedness, they will destroy with their character. As parents and spiritual leaders, we must raise the generations with a passion for training and a willingness to qualify at every level of play the Lord has ordained for them to play at.

The Kingdom is discovered

You can not inherit salvation nor can you inherit the Kingdom. Each person, each generation must discover the pearl of great price for themselves and then sell everything they have to buy it. Inheritance is never permitted to circumvent sacrifice, for it is the cost of selling everything to buy the Kingdom that produces the passion and zeal to keep seeking it. Therefore, we must lead our children into discovery of the Kingdom rather than taking them to the field and trying to dig the pearl up for them. If our children don't discover the Kingdom and buy it with their own money, they will sell out with no sense of the cost.

In Deuteronomy 6:10-12, we see this tension between spiritual inheritance and personal discovery. If left unchecked, spiritual inheritance produces a forgetfulness leading to apathy and entitlement and so Moses warns us to "Watch ourselves." The word watch in Hebrew means, "to build a hedge around, to guard as you would a flock." It is a very purposeful and intentional interaction that keeps an honor of what God has done, preventing any sense of entitlement or forgetfulness.

Parental leadership is the answer to entitlement. Parents who want to protect their children from the pitfalls of entitlement must:

A.   LEAD THEIR CHILDREN INTO DISCOVERY rather than give them all the answers. Generally speaking, is it much easier just to give answers, but in the long run answers only will rob the next generation from the joy and passion found in discovery. It was the joy of discovery that motivated the merchant to sell everything he had to buy the pearl of great price. Often people will come and ask me what I think their destiny is. I used to be quick to answer, thinking I was speaking destiny into their lives. However soon I noticed that those who ask would then run on the strength of what I saw for them rather than seeking God for a revelation for themselves. Now, I hint at what I see and then give some suggestions that will lead them into their own discovery and subsequent ownership.

B.   LEAD THEIR CHILDREN INTO ACTION rather than stopping at concepts. Conceptual truth is necessary to capture the children's imagination and set their course of pursuit. However, once the concepts have been clearly *yes*

defined, we must lead the generations into action. Action is what opens the door to significance. An opportunity for significance will prevent the pitfall of entitlement.

C. LEAD THEIR CHILDREN INTO A LIFESTYLE OF SACRIFICE. Never seek to alleviate the cost of buying the Kingdom. It was the price paid for truth that awakened the previous generation to the destiny that was theirs. Often in hopes to make it easier for the next generation, those who have gone before will eliminate the costs thinking they are doing the children a favor. The end result of this thinking is that they eliminate the very thing that made their generation what it was. The Puritans saw this reality in their forming of "the half-way covenant". In making it easier, they removed the need of God. In removing the need of God, they removed the avenue for grace.

We see the truth of this reality in Deuteronomy 7. In the first five verses Moses reminds the next generation what the cost of their coming into the land will be. Like the generation who had gone before, they would have to fight all the various inhabitants. Then Moses explained they would have to defeat issues that the forefathers did not have to. Due to the pitfalls of the next generation their areas of temptation would be to compromise and to lose their distinctions. It was this very fight for purity that was designed to awaken their destiny and stir the warrior in them. To alleviate the fight would have circumvented their course and thwarted their destiny.

2. FAMILIARITY. Like entitlement, familiarity is a pitfall of generational transfer. Familiarity was the sin of Esau. Like the entitlement of Jacob which caused him to think it nothing to lie for the birthright, the familiarity of Esau thought it nothing to trade the birthright away for a pot of stew. The aim of familiarity was not to steal the birthright. Its aim was to cause Esau to so devalue the worth of the birthright that he would be willing to give it away. Familiarity is an insidious enemy because by its very nature, you become familiar with your familiarity, so you are unaware of how much you have devalued the treasure you hold. In light of familiarity, the next generation will think nothing of neglecting the truths their parents gave everything for. It is not that they don't believe in those truths, it is just that the truths hold very little perceived value for them because they never fought the good fight to own them. This is why we as parents and

spiritual leaders must lead the next generation into the good fight of faith so they will come to understand the inherent value of truth. As we become intentional in expressing the inherent value of the truths we hold and lead the next generation in fighting for their own truths, we will neutralize the hold familiarity has had.

3. APATHY. Spiritual apathy is the natural outcome of someone in the hold of entitlement and familiarity. Entitlement and familiarity lead to the apathy of devotion. They produce the apathy of pursuit and the void of accomplishment. Many of the problems which youth get into today come, because they are spiritually bored. They live in a world of constant stimuli and over the top entertainment, and when it comes to the purposes of God they have been pacified with stories of greatness rather than being given opportunities for greatness. Over-stimulated and still bored are apt descriptions of many in the coming generation. To deal with this sense of boredom, the next generation must capture a sense of the awe and wonder of the Spirit led walk. Signs and wonders are the answer to the boredom they felt. If bored, then be used of God to raise someone from the dead and that will cure a good old fashion case of boredom. Our sons and daughters of the next generation, must be given opportunities for significance. They must be given a task, given a sphere to rule over and given a charge to lead. All of these combined will serve to dismantle the hold boredom has had. The next generation must be taught that serving Christ in the work of the Kingdom is the greatest adventure known to man. As devastating as apathy can be, it is always symptomatic of something far deeper. Apathy is the fruit of entitlement and familiarity. As we learn to dismantle the strongholds of entitlement and familiarity, apathy will suffer a death blow as well. With the roots torn up, the fruit will soon whither and spiritual life will suddenly return.

PRACTICAL PLANNING

As a whole, the purpose of *The Ancient Path* is to expound on the God given mandate of generational transfer. The success of any mandate will be defined by its plan. No planning is a plan to fail. A divinely inspired mandate followed by a divinely orchestrated plan will result in a secure future with a realistic hope. The remainder of this chapter is devoted to some of the practical tools we have used to facilitate generational joining and the awakening of generational passion. Two of the most important tools are Christ Church Academy and the Master's Commission which are described in further detail in the appendix.

The previous chapters have already spoken to the importance of fathers putting the children to bed at night, praying over them and evaluating their day. I have spoken of the importance of weekly times alone with each child to intentionally disciple them and guide their nurturing process. I have spoken of the importance of fathers "romancing" their daughters so their emotional cups are filled and they are not open to some young man looking to steal their innocence. Now in greater detail, I will address some tools for the teenage and pre-marriage years.

THE COVENANT OF PURITY

Protecting the purity of our children in an age of promiscuity is a very intentional task. Some would say it is nigh impossible. It is most definitely possible; it just requires persistent prayer and a strategic purpose. Two things we at Christ Church Kirkland have used quite effectively are The Covenant of Purity and Covenant Eyes. Covenant Eyes is a web site designed to report potential visits of undesirable internet sites. Once a user signs up, they choose a covenant partner and Covenant Eyes sends a list of any questionable sites visited. This list goes out once a week.

THE PURITY RING

Somewhere, around the age of 12 or 13, the father takes his son or daughter out to a formal dinner for the purpose of solemnizing the event. Both dress up to enhance the importance of the night. Over dinner, the father speaks to the child about the importance of purity, saving their virginity for their spouse, making a covenant with their eyes not to dwell upon unwholesome things. This could be the time fathers speak to their sons about "the facts of life." I would suggest it be the mother who describes this to the daughter. After a biblical vision for purity is layed out the father presents the child with a written covenant where the child covenants to remain pure and save their virginity for their spouse. The father writes this covenantal agreement in his own words and brings it to the dinner for both to sign. Once the covenant is signed, the father presents the child with a ring symbolizing that the child is under covenantal promise. The child remains under covenantal promise until the marriage covenant supersedes it.

The ring I gave my daughter Kelsey had seven small diamonds across the front of it. After her husband Jim gave her engagement ring, they had it redesigned with five diamonds flanking each side of her engagement solitaire. Her dream was to symbolize that her engagement was protected by her covenant to purity.

Undistracted Devotion

Space does not permit me to describe in detail how this covenant of purity is powered by a commitment to courtship as opposed to dating. The apostle Paul defined the biblical mandate of undistracted devotion in I Corinthians 7:35 *"to promote what is seemly and to secure undistracted devotion to the Lord."* With the goal of securing an undistracted devotion in the generations to come, we have encouraged parents to embrace the standard of courtship rather than dating. Statistics say the divorce rate is just as high in the church as it is in the world. In light of this reality, there must be a more kingdom way of forming relationships than the way the world has taught us to do so.

Through courtship, young people are asked to give their heart and devotion to no one except the Lord unless they feel this is the person they intend to marry. If two friends are just getting together socially, and not romantically, it is not considered a date. Potential "couples" get to know each other in groups and allow the foundation of their relationship to be built on friendship and not emotional entanglement.

In the ten years or so we at Christ Church Kirkland have encouraged the courtship process we have had more than 30 couples married with not a single divorce. In fact, I am not even aware of a couple who has had to have any type of ongoing counseling to sort out marital issues. Of course there have been relational conflicts, but the foundations laid in courtship allow for a much stronger ability to sort these conflicts out. When a couple builds their relationship on the foundations of friendship and does not introduce the physical until marriage, the issues of the heart are forced to develop and makes for a deeper ability to communicate.

RITES OF PASSAGE

One of the most powerful things we do at our church is a ceremony to bring our young boys into manhood and introduce them into the community of men. We call this ceremony "The Rites of Passage" or "The Walk of Fire." We are indebted to our good friend Dudley Hall in Texas who brought "The Rites of Passage" to us.

We do "The Rites of Passage" yearly in conjunction with our annual men's retreat. The retreat is held Friday evening through Saturday afternoon. All the men return at dusk for observance of the ceremony.

The rite actually begins several months earlier with an informational meeting of all potential candidates and their fathers. At this meeting, we state the purpose of "The Rites of Passage" and the responsibility of coming into the community of men. Eeach father is asked to read Robert Lewis' book *Raising a Modern Day Knight.* The fathers are instructed to begin a dialogue and journey with their sons on the subjects of integrity, responsibility and accountability. Each son is asked to write a one page paper on each subject and turn that paper in a week before the ceremony.

"The Rites of Passage" ceremony begins with an extended period of worship with all the men of the church. Those who will be going through the rites are then brought out into the church grounds where three tables are set up for each of the three subjects: integrity, responsibility and accountability. Behind each table is a leader from the church ready to ask the son to share what each word means to him. As the son comes to the table, he shares what the word means and is then given a bead with the single letter I, R or A printed on it. After each bead is received, the son leaves the table and is greeted by a group of men waiting to pray that subject over the boy. They then go to the table with the next word and duplicate the process until all three beads have been received and they are prayed over for all three.

The sons are then blindfolded by their fathers and led on "the walk of trust." This is just a blindfolded walk where the sons must listen to and trust their fathers for direction and protection. This walk leads them to one of the elders of the church who stands next to a lit tiki torch. By this time it is dark out and the tiki torches provide a great atmosphere of mystery and intrigue. The elder receives the three beads from the boy and puts them on a leather band. He shares with the boy concerning the responsibility of coming into the community of men. He then places the beads on the leather necklace and puts the necklace on the boy's neck. The boy then goes back into the sanctuary where he is prayed and prophesied over until all the boys have received their beads, gone on their walk of trust and talked to an elder and been prayed over.

In the meantime, each man has placed his tiki torch in 2 parallel lines about 100 feet long. The boys are then led to one end of the tiki torch lane while the fathers go to the other men. The men of the community line up on both ends to cheer on the walk. One by one the father comes to the end of the line of fire and calls out to his son to join the community of men. While a heart stirring soundtrack from "Braveheart" plays and all the men of the community cheer, the son walks the line of fire into the waiting embrace of is father.

This is an incredibly emotional ceremony that deeply marks the boys and men alike to the importance of being men and fathers in the Kingdom of God. The ceremonial aspect keeps it from becoming familiar or of no consequence.

ZIKLAG

Ziklag is another program at Christ Church Kirkland we use to underscore the importance and role of biblical manhood. Ziklag is a seven-week "boot camp" that combines physical and spiritual disciplines to define the role of men and recognize the fruit of a matriarchal society. Each participant commits to:

1. 30 minutes a day of Bible study
2. 30 minutes a day of prayer
3. Fasting once a week
4. Read 2 books

5. Write 3 papers
6. Meet once a week
7. Run 3 times a week

The participants meet once a week where they worship, share whether they fulfilled all the commitments, receive teaching and go on a run together. The subjects of the teaching are violence - in relationship to Matthew 11:12, courage, identity and destiny and endurance and discipline.

The purpose of Ziklag is to expose the stronghold of apathy over the typical Christian male and then awaken the warrior spirit.

More detailed information can be received on any of these tools by contacting us at 425.820.2900 or emailing us at office@cckirkland.org

It is imperative that parents accept the reality that godly seed requires intentional planning. The raising of rulers with divine connections wil be a costly investment that promises an eternal return.

RECOMMENDED READING

1. *Intercessory Prayer*, Dutch Sheets. Regal Books
2. *Dating Versus Courtship*, Paul Jehle. Plymouth Rocks Foundation
3. *Enemies From Within*, Norm Willis. Christ Church Publishing

FOOTNOTES

7. Strong's Concordance #430.
8. Ibid.

DISCIPLESHIP: *The* PATHWAY *to* GENERATIONAL JOINING

GENERATIONAL TRANSFER IS AUTOMATIC. For good or for ill, generational transfer happens. For that transfer to be positive, it must be purposeful and strategic. Children are born but disciples are made. They are made by a means of intentional training and strategic investment.

On any journey, a route must be determined to arrive at the intended destination. This route is intended to be traveled together, so the journey must begin with a mindset to keep the generations joined not separated. The Bible is written from an assumption of the generations joined together in Kingdom pursuit not separated into various age categories. Contemporary culture has given us children's church and youth church whereas the Bible just has church.

The Book of Acts describes everyone being together and having all things in common, but when we look at the contemporary way of having "church," we see everyone segregated into their like groups. The children have their meetings and the youth have theirs. We have singles groups, young married groups, seniors, professional and non-professional. It's not that these groups are inherently wrong, it's just that they promote generational segregation if they are not intentionally joined one to the other. For example, Christ Church Kirkland has a Wednesday night youth group but the fathers have joined the youth group, so that our youth focus is generationally joined not segregated.

Most definitely there are times and seasons when it is strategic to call an age group off to itself for specific training, but it should be done from the context of generational joining to the other generations.

THE PATHWAY DEFINED

Discipleship is the God-given pathway to generational transfer. The command to go and make disciples begins at home. Whether it be natural children or spiritual children, they must be made into disciples.

"Therefore go and make disciples of all nations, baptizing them in the name of the Father and of the Son and of the Holy Spirit, and teaching them in everything I have commanded you." (Matthew 28:19-20)

Contained in the words of Christ's command is a biblical strategy for generational transfer. God's eternal plan for generational joining was to transpire through the process of discipleship. Matthew 28:19-20 is the New Testament reiteration of the Dominion Mandate recorded in Genesis 1:28. Like divine bookends, these two mandates frame God's desire. The Dominion Mandate of Genesis 1 defines God's intent; the Great Commission of Matthew 28 defines His method. Both the intent and method are given as commands, therefore neither can be altered.

"God blessed them; and God said to them, "Be fruitful and multiply, and fill the earth, and subdue it; and rule over the fish of the sea and over the birds of the sky and over every living thing that moves on the earth." (Genesis 1:28)

It is often said, "The message is unchanging, but the method must adapt to the culture." Though this has a measure of truth, it is certainly not true when the method was given as a command and is central to the message. While many of our methods to advance the Kingdom can be separated from the message, discipleship cannot. Discipleship is both the message and the method. Since the method is commanded, it cannot be culturalized or dismissed. Discipleship is God's mandated method for world conquest.

The command to go and make disciples assumes two essential realities.

1. EVERY PERSON SHOULD BE A DISCIPLE — Because the law of reproduction is to reproduce after your own kind, to make disciples, you must first be a disciple. To teach others to obey everything Jesus commanded, we must first obey everything He commanded.) *good*

2. EVERY PERSON SHOULD BE DISCIPLING — The making of a disciple was not presented by Jesus as a suggestion; it was given as a command. The individual's responsibility to make disciples is the most basic command of New Testament expectation. Every believer is commanded by Christ to be actively discipled and to be actively making disciples.

DISCIPLESHIP DEFINED

The Greek word for "disciple" is "mathetes," meaning, "a learner." It comes from the root word "math" which carries three very significant definitions:

1. Thought accompanied by endeavor

> There is nothing conceptual about a disciple. Discipleship in its truest form must produce an endeavor. It will lead to action if it is biblical discipleship. How easy it is to think we are something once we have a conceptual understanding of it. There is a big difference between conceptual truth and actual truth. A disciple is one who stays in the process of advance until what they know becomes an endeavor.

2. Reception leading to implementation

> Implementation is the goal of discipleship, not mere knowledge. For a disciple, to know something is to implement what they know. If disciples do not implement what they think they know, they really do not know it.

3. Teaching followed by action

> The end result of these three definitions are all the same. They all end with demonstration. The three operative words in these definitions are endeavor, implementation, and action. Anybody can have thoughts, but a disciple has thoughts accompanied by endeavor. Anybody can receive truth, but a disciple has reception leading to implementation. Anybody can receive teaching, but a disciple must act on what they have been taught.

A disciple, by definition, is more than a pupil. A disciple is an adherent. A disciple is more than a student, a disciple is an imitator. A disciple can be identified by the imitation of the one they follow. *The Key Word Study Bible's Lexical Aid to the Old Testament*[9] says of the Greek Word "matheteuo," which is translated "disciple." "Matheteuo" means not only to learn, but to become "attached to one's teacher and become his follower in doctrine and conduct of life."[10]

The problem is, in our fiercely independent culture, that few are willing to imitate anybody, and those who do are looked upon with suspicion and cultic concerns. For the church to become all the church is intended to be, we must forsake our radical independence and return to the biblical pattern of discipling.

"If you hold to my teaching, then you really are my disciples."   (John 8:31)

Jesus seems to indicate that there are those who are "disciples," and then there are those who are "really disciples." To really be a disciple, there must be an intentional abiding in the Word. It requires a willingness to let the Word teach you, rebuke you, train you, and correct you. So, you can't be a disciple or make disciples unless you are willing to teach and be taught; rebuke and be rebuked; correct and be corrected; train and be trained.

"All Scripture is inspired by God and profitable for teaching, for reproof, for correction, for training in righteousness." (II Timothy 3:16)

"This is my Father's glory, that you bear much fruit, showing yourselves to be my disciples." (John 15:8)

A disciple is both a noun and a verb. A disciple is both a person and something that shows action. A disciple is someone who displays a posture of the heart and fruitfulness in his life. More than a title, discipleship is a description of something that transpires between two people.

A Discipleship Evaluation

Based upon these definitions of the word "disciple," are you one? How do you really know if you are a disciple? To know assuredly is to go back to the original definition.

> If by definition a disciple is one attached in doctrine and conduct to another, are you attached to anyone? Are you training your sons and daughters to be attached to you?

> If by definition, a disciple demonstrates thought accompanied by endeavors, is there fruit of endeavors in your life? Is there fruit of endeavors in your sons and daughter's life?

> If by definition, a disciple demonstrates reception leading to implementation, is there evidence of implementation in your life? Is there evidence of implementation in your sons and daughters?

> If by definition, a disciple is one who demonstrates teaching followed by action, are there signs of action in your life? Are there signs of action in

your sons and daughters?

You know you are a disciple by the level of endeavor, implementation, and action in your life. A biblical evaluation must also ask, "Are you making disciples?" Disciple-making is not a matter of specific calling. Disciple-making is a matter of universal obedience. Everyone is commanded to make disciples. In II Timothy 2:2, Paul defines the goal of the discipling process as the making of other disciples. The one being discipled is to advance their training by discipling others who in turn also disciple others, and so on and so forth. This process, of course, would begin in the home with your own sons and daughters and then extend to other spiritual sons and daughters the Lord might add.

"These things which you have heard from me in the presence of many witnesses, entrust these to faithful men who will be able to teach others also." (II Timothy 2:2)

SELF-MADE DISCIPLE

By definition, there is no such thing as a self-made disciple. Every disciple is made by someone else. The very command to "go and make disciples" signifies that disciples are not self-made. The pattern the Bible describes is one of making and being made. The pattern of disciple-making according to Matthew 28 and II Timothy 2 is everyone should be being made a disciple and also, be in the process of making disciples. If you are not in this process of being made a disciple or making other disciples, you really are not a disciple. "Being made" has to do with the willingness to be taught, molded, rebuked and trained. "Making disciples" involves the same. You can't possibly be a disciple if you are not willing to be called up and challenged. The same is true in regard to making disciples. For children to be made disciples they must be taught, directed, molded, rebuked and trained. Children left to themselves will very rarely become disciples.

THE FOUR STAGE PROCESS OF DISCIPLE-MAKING

The command to "go and make disciples" signifies an ongoing process of building. There are no "instant disciples." Disciples are built from the ground up. To be a disciple and to make disciples requires a willingness to stay in a process that takes you through various stages of growth and maturity. The biblical pattern seems to indicate a four-stage process. Though this is not an explicit pattern, the process can be seen. The pattern is not meant to be viewed as a program, but rather a process. The four stage process is:

1. Teaching
2. Mentoring
3. Training
4. Fathering

STAGE ONE: TEACHING

"Go and make disciples, teaching them to obey." (Matthew 28:19-20)

Teaching is the initial stage of the disciple-making process, for it establishes the disciple in the posture of the learner and lays biblical foundations properly. A disciple must be a learner who diligently gives themselves to a thorough understanding of basic foundations. In this initial stage of teaching, the disciple must learn the basic truths of:

> The nature of God
> The nature of man
> The nature of sin
> The necessity of salvation
> The nature of redemption
> Law and grace
> The work of the Holy Spirit
> The role of the church
> The necessity of community
> Spiritual gifts
> The exchanged life
> The fear of the Lord

If this foundational stage of teaching and learning is not laid properly, every other stage will reflect the error. In this initial stage of teaching, it is recommended you lead your natural and spiritual children through basic bible studies that focus on foundations and the truth mentioned above.

These could be your basic Navigator type "fill in the blank" Bible studies. This gets the student in the mindset of a seeker who is in search of the truth. This stage may require multiple years, depending on the speed of the individual's training.

KEY ATTITUDES OF THE DISCIPLE IN STAGE ONE OF TEACHING ARE:

> Discipline
> Hunger to learn
> Consistency
> Dependency
> Daily devotion
> Forgiveness

Recommended reading for stage one:

I. *The Foundations of the Christian Life*. Bob & Rose Weiner Maranatha Publications
2. *The Ultimate Intention*. Deverne Fromke. Sure Foundation
3. *The Normal Christian Life*. Watchman Nee Tyndale House Publications
4. *Grace Works*. Dudley Hall. Wire Books
5. *The Fear of the Lord*. John Bevere. Charisma House
6. *Playing God*. Norm Willis. Christ Church Publishing
7. *Vertical Reality*. Norm Willis. Christ Church Publishing

Some of these books are recommended in more than one stage, due to the comprehensiveness of their messages.

STAGE TWO: MENTORING

Mentoring is the second stage of the process where specific responsibility and proven accountability are introduced. Mentoring is the stage in the process where the disciple begins to be formed. Stage one gets the clay on the wheel; stage two begins to form the pot. In stage one the disciple receives a lot of information, stage two brings the disciple into transformation. It is in this stage wherein our disciple begins to own their faith for themselves. Teaching alone can result in substance without form.

Mentoring alone can produce form without substance. If you join the two together, you get substance with biblical form. It is in the stage of mentoring where we discover the jointedness of Christ's body according to Ephesians 2:21.

"In whom the whole building, being fitted together, is growing into a holy temple in the Lord." (Ephesians 2:21)

IN THIS SECOND STAGE OF MENTORING THE DISCIPLE MUST LEARN THE BIBLICAL TRUTHS OF:

> Covenant relationships
> Eternal purpose of God
> Purposeful living
> Individual calling
> Being self-initiating
> Being self-revealing
> Being self-governing
> Sonship
> The Kingdom of God

This stage requires a tremendous investment of time. It is recommended you set a weekly time of at least one hour to meet each one you a disciple. This may be a breakfast or lunch or some other configuration that is conducive to one on one, face to face interaction.

THE KEY ATTITUDES OF THE DISCIPLE IN THIS SECOND STAGE OF MENTORING MUST BE:

> Transparency
> Vulnerability
> Mold-ability
> Responsibility
> Integrity
> Humility

this is me

Don't be in a hurry to progress through various stages. Each stage takes as long as it takes. Be sensitive to the Holy Spirit for His affirmation of graduation.

Recommended reading for stage two:

1. *Covenant Relationships.* Keith Intrager. Destiny Image Publishers
2. *Ultimate Intention.* Deverne Fromke. Sure Foundations
3. *Normal Christian Life.* Watchman Nee. Tyndale House Publishers
4. *Under Cover.* John Bevere. Nelson Books
5. *Cost of Discipleship.* Detrich Bonhoffer. Touchstone
6. *That You May Prosper.* Ray Sutton. Institute for Christian Economics
7. *The Unshakable Kingdom the Unchanging Person.*
    E. Stanley Jones. McNett Press

STAGE THREE: TRAINING

Training is the third stage of the process where the disciple learns mastery. Stage three is where the apprentice graduates and becomes a journeyman. According to the proper foundations that were laid in teaching and the principles imparted in mentoring, the disciple is no longer a novice; he is now training how to come into a level of maturity and mastery.

"Study to show thyself approved, a workman who does not need to be ashamed, one who correctly handles the Word of Truth." (II Timothy 2:15)

In this passage, the Apostle Paul appeals to Timothy as a disciple. As a faithful father, he is pressing his spiritual son for mastery. As God's representatives on the earth, it is not enough to simply know what we know. To accurately represent God, we must become masters at what we know.

Michael Jordan, Tiger Woods, and Deion Sanders are all household names because they are masters at their craft. You can be good at something and still carry little influence in what you do. To be influential in your call, you must become a master at it.

IN THIS STAGE OF TRAINING THAT THE DISCIPLE MUST LEARN THE MASTERY OF:

> Kingdom values
> Calling and placement
> Leadership and influence
> Problem-solving
> Gift development

- > Carrying another's heart
- > Biblical worldview
- > Legislative prayer
- > Prophetic leading

THE KEY ATTITUDE OF THE DISCIPLE IN THIS THIRD STAGE OF TRAINING MUST BE:

- > Diligence
- > Faithfulness
- > Availability
- > Follow-through
- > Time management

RECOMMENDED READING FOR STAGE THREE:

1. *Seven Habits of Highly Effective People.* Stephen R. Covey. Free Press
2. *Spiritual Leadership.* Henry Blackaby
   Broadman and Holman Publishers
3. *Thinking Straight in a Crooked World.* Gary DeMar. American Vision
4. *Assumptions that Affect Our Lives.* Christian Overman
   Micha 6:8 Publishing
5. *When God Speaks.* Chuck Pierce. Regal Books
6. *Treasure in the Field.* Brian Watts. Imogen Resources
7. *When Heaven Invades Earth.* Bill Johnson. Treasure House

STAGE FOUR: FATHERING

The ultimate goal of the disciple-making process is Christ-likeness and fatherhood. Fathering is the stage before reproduction takes place.

"Even though you have ten thousand guardians in Christ, you do not have many fathers, for in Christ Jesus I became your father through the Gospel." (I Corinthians 4:15)

The reason there are so few fathers in the faith is that few are willing to stay in the process that enables them to become fathers. There has been an unwillingness to pay the price, offenses, private agendas, and sin. These and others are all reasons why the process gets circumvented and the fathers are prevented from emerging. More than a title, fatherhood is a description. A father is a father not because he calls himself one, but because his life has been reproduced into the life of another. The true essence of fatherhood is the transferring of one's heart and way into the life of another. It's not about the transferring of one's personality, but the transferring of God's life and call into the son and daughter He has placed in your life.

Fathering is the stage in our discipling process when we learn to do for others what has been done for us. Through the impartation of fathering, the Holy Spirit reproduces the deposit of God in one generation into the heart of the generation to follow. Like Elijah to Elisha, often that reproduction carries with it a double portion anointing.

It's in this final stage of fathering that we really learn what we thought we always knew. Studies show you really don't know something until you know it well enough to teach others. Statistics reveal some pretty staggering facts in regard to comprehension and retention rates. Though the exact percentages may vary from person to person, most show we comprehend and retain:

> 5% of what we read
> 10% of what we hear
> 30% of what we see
> 80% of what we experience
> 95% of what we teach

In the reproduction of truth, there is great comprehension and retention.

It is in the fourth stage of fathering that the disciple must learn the eternal truths of:

> Generational joining
> Generational transfer
> Inheritance of the heart
> Success found in succession
> Power of impartation

The key attitudes of the disciple in the fourth stage of fathering must be:

> Christ-likeness
> Selflessness

> A father's heart
> A servant's heart
> Patience
> Purity
> Representation

RECOMMENDED READING FOR STAGE FOUR:

1. *You have not many fathers.* Dr. Mark Hanby. Destiny Image.
2. *Family man, family leader.* Philip Lancaster. The Vision Forum.
3. *Raising a modern day knight.* Robert Lewis. Focus on the Family.

Someone once said, "The concern of Jesus was not with the programs to reach the multitudes, but with the people whom the multitudes would follow." To prepare such a people, our children must be taught, mentored, discipled, and fathered.

A disciple is one willing to stay before the Holy Spirit's continual evaluation.

"Test yourselves to see if you are in the faith; examine yourselves! Or do you not recognize this about yourselves, that Jesus Christ is in you, unless indeed you fail the test?" (II Corinthians 13:5)

> Are you being taught?   Are you teaching?
> Are you being mentored?   Are you mentoring?
> Are you being discipled?   Are you discipling?
> Are you being fathered?   Are you fathering?

The process of disciple-making never stops. Even when it appears that the basic stages are complete, the necessity of increase and advance remains. David is our example in this reality. On his death bed, even when his son Solomon was king, David was still fathering. His last words were *"Show yourself the man..." (I Kings 2:2)* Even in death David was still fathering his son and Solomon was receiving it.

Practical Outworking of Discipleship

Though Jesus made clear the command to make disciples, He didn't explain the practical steps as to how those disciples should be made. Consequently, there are a multitude of ideas, most of which have merit. More than defining an exact step-by-step process that must be followed, wisdom is to develop a process that is workable between the leader and the one being discipled. This plan should be specific and it should be consistent. To bring a disciple through the stages of teaching to fathering requires regular one-on-one meetings of instruction, formation, and assignment. A weekly meeting is optimum, or at least a bi-weekly meeting.

The previous suggestions of what must be learned in each stage provide a format of topics to discuss during the meeting process. Genuine discipleship is a mutually-defined relationship of accountability and life formation recognized by two parties. Simply getting together each week for coffee is not necessarily discipleship. Discipleship, by definition, must involve certain practices for it to be genuine discipleship. A disciple is defined by the fruit of their life. For there to be fruit, there must be certain aspects transpiring in the relationship.

Qualities to instill in the discipleship process

1. Full Disclosure of Heart and Behavior

"But if we walk in the light, we have fellowship with one another, and the blood of Jesus His Son purifies us from all sin." (I John 1:7)

Please notice how our relationship to Jesus is inseparably linked to our disclosure with our brother. The spirit of discipleship is volunteerism. Consequently, there must be a full willingness to walk in the light without any hint of coercion. Full disclosure of the heart means no hidden sins, no private agendas, and no false fronts. This of course is a trained response that requires time. Be patient, but be intentional.

The key to full disclosure is the heart of both the disciple and the discipler. If either are not in the process with a whole heart, knowing God has ordered the process, it will go astray. Without heart, the process will be perceived as control. Discipleship will flourish only in the presence of willingness of heart and the openness of one's life. To come into mastery, the disciple must let the discipler into their inner conversations, fears, dreams, etc. We are not meant to carry all these things alone.

"Bear one another's burdens, and thereby fulfill the law of Christ." (Galatians 6:2) This, of course, is far easier for the natural son or daughter than it is for the spiritual son or daughter especially if from a small age the father has been taking the child out on "weekly dates." When this has transpired the child is quite accustomed to opening up to the parent. If this condition is not your reality, read on, there is hope.

2. Genuine Accountability

"Obey your leaders and submit to their authority. They keep watch over you as men who must give an account" (Hebrews 13:17)

The way of the Lord is the way of interdependence. The Body of Christ is an interdependent Body made up of joints and relationships that cause the Body to build itself up in love.

In whom the whole building, being fitted together, is growing into a holy temple in the Lord, in whom you also are being built together into a dwelling of God in the Spirit." (Ephesians 2:21-22)

If we could have reached mastery and fatherhood alone, Jesus could have just given us a Bible and never instituted the church. But, Jesus birthed the church and fitted and framed us together so that we could call each other up into maturity and keep each other accountable.

Accountability is not for the purpose of creating a subservient relationship. Accountability is designed for the purpose of calling us up, not keeping us down. Someone might ask, "Do I really need accountability?" The answer to that question depends on what one intends to accomplish. If one does not intend to accomplish anything, accountability is not necessary. On the other hand, if someone intends on accomplishing great things, accountability is essential. To fulfill our God-given destiny, we must do so according to the biblical pattern, and accountability is an essential element of that pattern. For those discipling their own children, this accountability would begin in how they spend time with Jesus, steward their belongings, care for their relationships, respect authority, do their homework, etc,.

3. Mastery of Kingdom Principles

"Everyone who competes in the games goes into strict training." (I Corinthians 9:25)

The mastery of Kingdom principles does not come naturally. There is a strict training required to accomplish mastery, and discipleship is the God-ordained structure for that training to transpire.

In order to reach that level of mastery, you must "declare your major." Like one studying for a degree, you must know the subject you will get your degree in. You will never master your calling without clearly discerning the specific aspects of that call. Many never reach the level of mastery, because they never specialize their training. Parents must help their children discern that God given call so they can specialize their training.

If your calling is a business, you must specialize your training in business principles and master your field. If your call is in politics, master the political process. If the pastoral realm is your call, embrace the training necessary to become a master in that field. If homemaking is the call then find the help of the Holy Spirit to make that spiritual oasis.

Discipleship is the God-ordained structure to assist you in that training. Discipleship is to help you discern your specific call, and equip you to master that call. It is also the pathway enabling you to reproduce that life in others.

4. Reproduction of Your Life and Pursuits

"The things you heard me say in the presence of many witnesses, entrust to faithful men who will also be qualified to teach others." (II Timothy 2:2)

Reproduction is a basic expectation of the Christian life. The command to go and disciple the nations is a universal command. It is not limited to age, gender, or maturity. Regardless how little or how much, whatever has been given you must be turned over. If it is kept, it will be lost, but if it is given away, it will return with increase.

Resolve It

To fulfill the command of discipleship, it will require us to resolve certain obstacles.

1. Obstacle of Personal Exemption — This is the cheap grace some give themselves not to go and make disciples, for they think the command does not apply to them. If you have children it absolutely applies to each of them. If you have been entrusted with truth, it becomes your responsibility

to pass that truth on to others according to II Timothy 2:2.

2. OBSTACLE OF TIME MANAGEMENT — There is no way around it; to make disciples requires time. The good news is that we have enough time. The same twenty-four hours a day given to Jesus has been given to us. If He could disciple His twelve to turn the world upside down with only twenty-four hours, so can we. Time is meant to be spent, not saved. Rather than looking for opportunities to "save time," why not look to spend it?

IN CONCLUSION

The making of disciples is not an option; it is a command. Discipleship is the God-ordained means by which we are brought into the fullness of our destiny, and to train others to come into the fullness of theirs. Children are born, disciples are made. If you will begin discipling your children from an early age they will know their God and do exploits for His Kingdom.

WHY IS THIS TRUTH SO IMPORTANT TO US?

> It is the God-given means to come into mastery of our Kingdom call.
> It is the God-given means for the purpose of generational joining and generational transfer.
> It fulfills the basic obedience to biblical commands.
> It is the means by which the saints are equipped to do the work of ministry.
> It is the God-given strategy for cultural dominion.

TAKE A STEP

I. Have the one you disciple write a three page paper answering these questions:

> Who am I?
> Why am I here?
> Where am I going?

2. After discussion and fine tuning of these questions, have them answer a follow up question.

> How will I get there?

3. Discern what stage (teaching, mentoring, training, fathering) your disciple is at. Then map out a plan to instill the truth of that next level.

> Assign books to read.

> Assign papers to write.

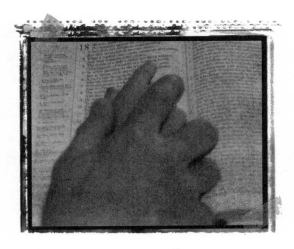

Appendix

It may prove helpful to describe some of the practical methods we employ to assure the process of generational transfer. These are explained only as an example of what could be done to secure the future of the generations to come. They are in no way the only means or even the best means; they are simply alternatives. What is essential is that the process of generational transfer is accomplished whatever the means you employ to do so.

The Master's Commission

The Master's Commission is a one-year, full-time, discipleship-training program for men and women approximately between the ages of 18 and 25. It serves as a one-year "boot camp" of intense character training to prepare each student for a life of servanthood, sonship and ministry, that they might be *"...vessels of honor, sanctified, useful to the Master and prepared to do any good work." (II Timothy 2:21)*

The Master's Commission is an opportunity for all students to deepen their relationship to Jesus Christ by abandoning themselves to the pursuit of the Kingdom of God, expressed through the disciplined lifestyle of undistracted devotion, prayer, worship, Bible study, and community service.

The core values of The Master's Commission are as follows:

1. Personal intimacy with Jesus
A daily, vital relationship with Jesus Christ, expressed through devotional prayer, worship, and Scripture memorization, is the cornerstone of The Master's Commission. Each student will be led into the joy of personal intimacy with Christ and the art of discerning His voice.

2. Character building
Believing that what they build with their giftedness, they can easily destroy with their character, The Master's Commission makes character development its primary focus. Through a thorough curriculum of study and heart application, students are challenged to submit more fully to the Holy Spirit, those in authority over them, and to their fellow students.

3. Servanthood

Those who serve, lead. Students of The Master's Commission are taught leadership through practical avenues of service to the body of Christ. Pregancy help clinics, the City of Kirkland Parks and Recreation departmen, janitorial work, aiding the elderly, work in the inner city and serving the staff at Christ Church Kirkland all examples of this service.

4. Biblical Worldview Studies

To become sound in doctrine and in the understanding of God's Word is a goal of The Master's Commission. This is accomplished through daily study of the Bible. In addition, each student will study and learn to prepare lessons to teach from books of relevant truth with anointed content.

5. Covenant Relationship.

Understanding the importance of relationships in the body of Christ and learning how to relate together according to covenantal principles is a must. Relationships that will last a lifetime and continue on into eternity are forged together in The Master's Commission. Ministry of the Holy Spirit and the leadership of the Holy Spirit in each believer's life is of paramount concern to The Master's Commission. Much time is spent on the discovery and maturing of spiritual gifts and the ability to follow the Holy Spirit's leading.

6. Sonship

The students of The Master's Commission are taught the value of spiritual genes. They are trained to recognize the distinctives of the spiritual family they were placed in and honor the spiritual father given to them.

THE BENEFITS OF THE MASTER'S COMMISSION:

1. The privilege of giving one year full-time service to the Kingdom of God and the local church.

2. To bridge the gap between high school and college career by providing focus of disciplined training and pursuit of destiny.

3. To be equipped for ministry, vocation, and everyday life through practcal experience and servant leadership.

4. The development of academic disciplines is enhanced through an emphasis on personal study habits, written and oral communication skills, and Scriptural studies.

THE COMMITMENT OF THE MASTER'S COMMISSION:

1. Devotion
The Master's Commission student commits to one year of undistracted devotion, during which they give up jobs, dating, or any other practice that would serve as a possible distraction to the pursuit of Jesus Christ.

2. Housing
The Master's Commission students live with a host families from the church who agree to cover their room and board for the year they are in the program.

3. Schedule
Tuesday - Friday 7:30am - 5:00pm. Morning is spent in worship, prayer and Bible teaching. Saturdays and Sundays are scheduled as events unfold. Mondays are scheduled as a day off.

4. Tour of Ministry
To become doers of the Word is the intent of The Master's Commission. After eleven months of training and character development, the remaining time is spent travelling throughout the nation or internationally in ministry and demonstration of what they have learned.

For further information about The Master's Commission, write or e-mail us at:
The Master's Commission
Christ Church Kirkland
11725 NE 118th St
Kirkland, WA 98034
(425) 814.6303
E-mail: masters@cckirkland.org / Web: www.masterscommission.org

CHRIST CHURCH ACADEMY VISION STATEMENT

We have been given a mandate as a church to raise up "cultural reformers." Like the sons of Issachar who understood their times, our children will know what they were born to do. (I Chronicles 12:32). We believe the Classical Christian Model of Education is one of the tools God has shown us to equip and train our young people to become all that God created them to be in their generation. By the time they graduate they will be able to know what they believe, to write and speak intelligently about who they are, where they came from, what God is doing in the earth, and why they are here at this time in history with a passionate heart to do it.

We believe the Scripture is clear in Deuteronomy 6 about passing on a multi-generational godly heritage onto the next generation. This is to take place first in the home by parents modeling Christ-like character through the impartation of true wisdom, revelation, understanding, righteousness, justice, discretion, knowledge, and dependence upon God, in order that they would be equipped for life with the character and passion of Christ. We also want to help train them to become self-governing under the Lordship of Jesus and effective in every aspect of service bringing the Kingdom of God into every situation they are sown into.

We believe the pathway into this kind of lifestyle of abandonment is a serious surrender to the person of Jesus Christ. This is only imparted through the Holy Spirit as He reveals the love and justice of Father God and our Savior and King – Christ Jesus.

We believe the five-fold giftings of the church are to be joined together with the parents to help equip them in the biblical mandate of teaching and training their children.

We see a covenant community of godly parents and children embracing the purpose they were born for. To "rule and take dominion of the earth" under the Lordship of Jesus Christ in every sphere and jurisdiction of society. (Genesis 1:26-28) We see that when we understand and train ourselves and our children in the "ways of the covenant" – in time – "the earth will be filled with the glory of the Lord." We believe this type of education will produce young people who truly "understand the times" and know what they have been born for and how to do it.

We endeavor to be faithful to what has been shown us in our generation and pass it on to our seed that they may take it further than we have ever dreamed. For His glory alone!

Christ Church Academy was founded in 1992 out of a desire to return to the Ancient Path of parental responsibility in the mandate of education. There is nothing unique in home schooling but, what makes this school unique is its *cooperative* nature. Christ Church Academy combines the curriculum of a home school with the shared resources of its local church, Christ Church Kirkland. Consequently, the children do not suffer when their learning level surpasses the knowledge of their parents.

Christ Church Academy is overseen by "The Trustee of the Vision," who serves to place the parents of the co-op into the classrooms according to their area of expertise and passion. These parents then serve as classroom overseers who help the students, while not usurping the responsibility of the students parent. The parent always maintains the burden of responsibility for the respective child, while the eldership of the local church carries the government of the whole. The co-op is done in the facility of Christ Church Kirkland, Monday through Thursday, with Friday being a home-school day.

VISION STATEMENT

Proverbs 1:2-7; 23:6; Deuteronomy 6:6-9; Ephesians 4:11-12

> To pass a godly heritage on to the next generation through the impartation of true wisdom, revelation, understanding, righteousness, justice, prudence, discretion, knowledge and dependence upon God, in order that they would be equipped for life, made dynamic in service, and powerful in ministry.

> To see the five-fold gifting of the church joined together with the parents in order to equip them in the biblical mandate of teaching and training their children.

GOAL STATEMENT

Proverbs 1; I Chronicles 12:32; II Timothy 2:15

> With wisdom, anointing, and building upon the foundation of the Holy Spirit and biblical absolutes, parents and church staff will work together to:

1. Instill in each student the fear of God, knowing that the fear of God is the beginning of wisdom.
2. Train students to be godly in character: respectful of authority, kind, humble, well mannered, decisive, punctual, and responsible.
3 Nurture students in the art of self-discipline in order to prepare them to be motivated in life.
4. Equip each student with a complete, Spirit-filled, academic foundation, including Bible, Language Arts, Mathematics, Science, Social Studies, and Fine Arts.

> In cooperation with parents, our expectation is that each student will:

1. Possess a biblical worldview.
2. Know how to be spiritual self-feeders.
3. Discern what God has created them to be and do.
4. Develop their own unique expressions of heart-felt worship to God.
5. Learn how to be problem-solvers in a world of problem-makers.
6. Know how to discern the voice and leading of the Holy Spirit.

Philosophy Statement

I Corinthians 1:18-2:16

> Christ Church Academy exists to bring together the special giftings of parents enabling Christ Church Kirkland students to receive a superior and unique education. We hope to provide the latitude children need as they learn, instill godly character and respect of authority, and give each student the opportunity to discover and use their God-given gifts.

> The education of our children will be built upon the foundation of the Holy Spirit. Recognizing that the natural man cannot receive the things of the Spirit of God because they are spiritually discerned, we will seek to instill truth that is taught by the Spirit, and expressed in spiritual words.

Implementation Statement

Deuteronomy 6:6-9; Malachi 4:6; Ephesians 6:4

> Fathers will be the key to implementing this vision; and, with the equipping of the church, they will provide the necessary motivation and discipline for their children.

> By the power of the Holy Spirit, parents and pastoral staff will build true academic education upon the foundation of spiritual passion through daily times of prayer, worship, meditation, and Bible study.

> With the equipping of the church and the oversight of a Master Teacher, parents will teach the students and provide necessary supervision to guarantee that they comprehend the material taught.

> Students will not be limited to the pace of their age or grade level, but will proceed at the pace of their own learning abilities.

DISCIPLINE AND MOTIVATION

> Fathers are the key to implementing the vision. (Malachi 4:6) They supply the necessary motivation and discipline for their children.

> Pastoral equipping for parents—One meeting per month (Sunday night).

TRAINING THINKERS AND PROBLEM SOLVERS

> Students are shown how to master the process and apply concepts, not just learn facts. *"Knowledge puffs up."* They are being trained to be problem solvers—people who understand the times and can make a difference in the world. (II Chronicles 12:32)

> Students learn research skills, note-taking, outlining, study skills, and how to apply critical thinking.

PARENTAL INVOLVEMENT AND RESPONSIBILITY

> The parents are the teachers. Nine hours per week per family in areas of giftedness.

FOR INFORMATION ON STARTING A CLASSICAL CHRISTIAN SCHOOL, PLEASE CONTACT CHRIST CHURCH ACADEMY AT: 425.823.4307

Strategic Life Training

Strategic Life Training is a "training" course designed to prepare young Christians to lead in their generation. It focuses on both theory and practice in order to fully equip people to face and overcome today's and tomorrow's challenges. We believe that God desires to raise a new generation of Christian leaders, believers called to be Josephs and Esthers in their communities and nations. We believe that the Bible is abundantly clear on how to meet every need that the future holds.

Strategic Life Training is designed to teach Christian young people the truth of God's Word and to train them to walk in the freedom it provides. We are equipping Christians who will successfully address the challenges of tomorrow. We are challenging people to become leaders, embracing internal changes, that external change might begin.

Strategic Life Training is designed to equip the believer where God has called them and for the situations to which He has called them. The program focuses on teaching a Christian worldview, implementing a disciple's lifestyle, leadership training, Biblical problem solving, mentor-based accountability and community service.

This two-year correspondence course is designed to become a part of the lifestyle of those participating. In the first year of the program, interns are equipped to think biblically as they study presuppositional thinking, Christian worldview, and biblical ways of addressing current problems. In the second year of the program, interns are challenged to a disciple's lifestyle as they cultivate a life of "offense" and develop a sensitivity to God's plan for maturing them.

Strategic Life Training is mentor-based and relational. It is built upon an assumption that God trains us in the context of His relationship with us and those He has brought into our lives. It is built upon the assumption that God builds generationally and desires to see wisdom, understanding and knowledge transferred and shared generationally. Every intern has a mentor who keeps him/her accountable to apply the material to their lives, adding counsel and life experience to the books and tapes for maximum impact.

It all begins with a regional intensive where people from all specic regions gather for great teaching, relational building and a lot of fun!

Then the curriculum begins with weekly assignments, designed for training in godly principles and actions. Each year interns apply what they are learning to service projects designed to bring genuine change to the communities in which God has placed them.

Strategic Life Training was founded in 1991 by Dennis Peacocke. The program has since been established internationally, with schools in New Zealand and Europe. It is an incredible opportunity for training young leaders to be "pillars" in their families, churches, and communities; to equip the next generation to run the race to win, and to give their lives for effective and impacting service to God. Strategic Life Training provides leadership training for life, whatever the specific occupation, position or situation. It provides incredible opportunities for impact through service projects, summer schools, regional meetings, summer trips, leadership conferences and internships. Most importantly, it trains for the fulfillment of the destiny for which they were created, called, and placed by God.

Bibliography

Mansfield, Stephen. *Never Give In, The Extraordinary Character of Winston Churchill.* Highland Books, Elkton, MD, 1995.

Peacocke, Dennis. *Almighty and Sons: Doing Business God's Way.* Rebuild, Santa Rosa, CA, 1995.

Hicks, Robert. *The Masculine Journey,* Nav Press.

Kylstra, Chester and Betsy. *Restoring the Foundations: Counseling by the Living Word.* Proclaiming His Word, Inc., Santa Rosa Beach, FL, 1994.

Hanby, Doctor Mark. *You Have Not Many Fathers.* Destiny Image Publishers, Shippensburg, PA, 1997.

DeVern, F. Fromke. *Ultimate Intention.* Fure Foundation, Indianapolis, IN, 1993.

QTY:

☐ Ancient Path $16.00

☐ Vertical Reality..$16.00

☐ Unity With A Return - BOOK & CD $10.00

☐ Unity With A Return - BOOK & TAPE $10.00

☐ Playing God $5.00

☐ Enemies from Within $5.00

☐ Unfriendly Fire $5.00

*Add $5.00 for orders totaling less than $30.00
For all orders over $30.00 please call for shipping

SUBTOTAL $ ———————

*PLUS SHIPPING & HANDLING $ ———————

TOTAL $ ———————
(Prices include WA State sales tax)

Name: _____

Address: _____

_____

Phone: _____

Please mail your order with a check to:
Christ Church Publishing
11725 Ne 118th St, Kirkland, Wa 98034
Phone: 425.820.2900 Fax: 425.820.5627
Email: publishing@cckirkland.org

THE *Ancient* PATH[II]